Letters to Mack 2

Correspondence from Montana to Montauk

By Tom McCoy

Author of **How to Fly Fish for Trout:**
The First Book to Read

Cover and Back Photos: A striped bass blitz off the Montauk lighthouse.

Dedication

To all my fishing friends
who have made these stories possible

A digital edition is available on Kindle.com
Wholesale inquiries at Createspace.com

Table of Contents

Introduction 1

1. **When You Give You Get** 7
2. **April Trout** 13
3. **May Trout** 23
4. **June Trout** 31
5. **July Trout - A Western Journal** 41
6. **Putnam Pond** 57
7. **Hannah** 61
8. **Catskills in June** 69
9. **Missoula to Jackson** 79
10. **4 AM with the Boys** 103
11. **Four Peaks** 109
12. **Twin Ponds** 127
13. **Shared Waters** 129
14. **Missoula to Yellowstone by way of the Big Hole** 135
15. **Montauk on a Fly** 149
16. **Jerry** 157
17. **Negley Farson** 163
18. **Adirondack Reprieve** 169
19. **The Walk** 175

About the Author 179
Books by Tom McCoy 181

Introduction

Letters to Mack, Book One covered a wide variety of
fishing from fly fishing on streams to bunker snagging and
bottom fishing in the salt. As the years have moved on, the
desire to do more fly fishing has bumped the bait fishing
down to a little fluking and perhaps some black fishing in
the fall. Trying a fly on blue fish in the first book marked
the beginning of a new era for Tom. These days he heads
out with fluke bait in the cooler but will always take a few
casts with his ever-ready 9 weight at Winkle Point or over
at Duck Island, maybe even in Huntington Harbor after
gassing up. The result is that the fluke bait doesn't get a
chance to thaw as the stripers come over the side, a lead-
eyed, green and white streamer in the corner of the mouth.

Tom's home waters, when it comes to trout, are the
Catskills of New York so it is appropriate that the first
stories in this collection take place there. Living on the
Long Island Sound and being a short distance from the

saltwater mecca of Montauk, he has been fortunate to fish there as well; a witness to the amazing triple play of bass, blues and false albacore, all exploding at once within the shadow of the famous lighthouse.

Fly fishermen have a need to look west, beyond the prairies. Montana and its sister states with their mountains, wild streams and monster trout have been the magnet which has drawn Tom for many years. He offers a journal of three of those trips for your vicarious fishing pleasure.

All of these stories were written as letters to his lifelong friend Mack. "Sometimes you have the good fortune to meet a buddy early on and get to share your life with him" said Tom. "At first it's in school or on the ball field and later through correspondence. Letters at first, then email."

Letters to Mack 2: Correspondence from Montana to Montauk is a collection of 19 of those letters. From fishing adventures to deeply moving thoughts of friends, family and life, this book gives a little deeper look into who Tom is as an angler, and as a human being.

The Introduction from **Letters to Mack, Book One**:
Correspondence on a Fishing Life:

2014

So who is Mack?

Mack is my friend. We met in 1953 thanks to the Delaney
Card System and the need to alphabetize all those baby
boomers. We shared a seat as there were not enough desks
for all the new arrivals at the school which was only half
built. We walked home together, I was Cypress and he
was Cobalt (or was it Cottonwood?), more alphabetic
mania, this time by Mr. Levitt. We were limited to seeing
each other during school for the two blocks were a world
away from each other.

As we grew the neighborhood shrunk. We played sand lot
and army, eventually football and lacrosse together. We
watched the 1958 World Series eating peanut butter on
saltines and thinking we were in heaven. His Mom
bought a ski boat in 1962 and we spent hours on Oyster
Bay, returning to eat them out of house and home. Then
there was surfing and drinking and girls and drinking and
cars and drinking.

He had it tougher at home than I did. My Dad might have
been strict, but his wasn't there. His Mom was a proud
Irishman who held her head high, working at the high
school and keeping the household together. He spent a lot

3

of time on my bedroom floor, so much so that my Mother would ask where he was when not at dinner in the years before he went to service. We shared all of our secrets in the dark of that room. We were closer than brothers.

He joined the Air Force, became a heavy equipment operator and they sent him to Nam, Red Horse Battalion. We corresponded regularly. He sent an audio tape with the bombs going off in the background during the Tet Offensive. He sent photos of himself in fatigues near the perimeter. We wrote. Sue got to know him through the letters and she wrote back as well. That is when it all began, my letters to Mack.

When he returned, I was away doing my Navy time. He married and began a family. He was working at a tire store, had a new Buick and an apartment at the in-laws so they could save money. It looked as if he was going to live the American dream.

When I returned and was struggling, he was there to support me. He had a truck run upstate to deliver snow tires. I forget what it paid but he had me come along so he could split it with me. The truck broke down on the way back, but that's another story.

I went back to school and he moved into a house out east and we saw each other less. I lost him for about 10 years, although he was on my mind. We just didn't make the time to reach out.

In the 80's we got together again. I forget how, but we

found each other. Lots of things had happened. He had 3 kids, moved to a nicer home and was driving a new Honda. It was immaculate as all his cars always were and are today. We had both gotten back into fishing and shared the passion and stories. He was having some difficulty with domestic life.

We had lunch and he bared his soul about his Mother and her death, his bout with booze and his crazy thoughts. I was stunned as he was mirroring thoughts I had had and talked of things that I was struggling with as well. Then he disappeared.

Fast forward to 1996, the spread of the internet and online services. I get a letter with the usual misspellings and unique hand writing which read "If you are the Tom McCoy who grew up in Westbury…" I called immediately. He had found me in an on line directory and guessed that if the address was near water it had to be me. We laughed and cried and shouted at each other. When I hung up Sue said "Who was that?" a bit miffed by my instant maturation regression. "It was Mack" is all I said, with a big smile on my face.

He divorced shortly after we last were together and was in Las Vegas for the last 10 years and doing okay. He built a high end house cleaning business. He seemed happy. We began our correspondence again, first with letters and then by email. I went to Vegas on a business trip and we spent the weekend getting reacquainted.

Since that time we have been in regular contact with each

other and taken a few fishing trips together, some here, some out west. He writes of his kayaking and camping, his trout trips to the Truckee and into Utah. More recently he moved to Oregon. I write of my time on the boat and trout trips with Jerry, about the job and life.

We are again sharing our inner most secrets with each other as we did in the dark room we shared back on Cypress Lane. He came east immediately when I had a particularly ugly career bump. I went there as he hit some tough times. We both went through a bit of cancer. He has had heart problems and more, cared for by the VA. PTSD has taken a part of his soul for sure.

Our friendship is about being there for one another, both knowing that our relationship is a forever thing and not to be broken by our mutual misbehaviors or the happenings of the world around us or the miles between us.

So that is who Mack is, my friend, and these are some of the letters.

Chapter One

When You Give You Get

2005

Mack,

Ever since my grandson was born, in mid-May, our annual
fishing trip has slipped to a later date. At first it was a
disappointment since the mid-May period was preferred
due to the Hendrickson hatch. On the other hand it was
often cold, sometimes it snowed, high water was common
and there never were all that many fish. This year we went
the last week in May and were pleasantly surprised with
the weather, the water and the insects, not to mention the
fish. I think we have been kidding ourselves all these
years that early is better.

It was Moe, Jerry, Manny and I who planned to go. We asked Mickey as well but the golf bug has bitten him hard. At first we were all to drive up in Manny's Suburban but then Moe had a commitment and later Manny had to delay his departure. So Jerry and Moe drove up on Sunday afternoon and I came by myself early Sunday. Manny joined us on Monday. It all worked out.

I don't mind time in the car and got in a few hours of fishing before they arrived. We were in the same cabin as last year. There were rumors that the recent flood had damaged the camp but it barely got to the porches. The flow in front of the cabin, where there was always a rising fish, has been blocked by tons of river rock making a backwater of what was an active branch of the stream.

I started on the riffle just below the cabin. Before I knew it, Jerry and Moe were on the stream next to me. We fished a while with no luck, although there were a few rises. Jerry eventually brought up a fish on a nymph. A good sign. It was cold and rainy and I decided to go in for a breather.

Once warmed up, I headed to the pool above the camp. It is a long walk through shallow riffles but is said to hold some big trout.

I got up there and was alone. I waded to mid-stream as the rises in the past had been toward each bank. Rather than blind cast I waited, 4:30 and rain. No rises. 5:30 still no rises. Then a splash behind me, and one in front, one upstream and one down. The fish suddenly woke up.

I searched the water to see what they might be taking and saw tiny blue wing olives and some caddis. I tried the caddis as I could see it, but no takers. I searched my fly box and found what looked like a blue wing olive in a larger size than was on the stream. It had a tall CDC wing so I could see it. For me it was better to fish with a fly I could see than trying to use one that matched the hatch but was invisible under these conditions.

The fish were not rising consistently. There seemed to be a pattern of two or three rises and then none. I may have been putting them down with my casting so I waited for a fresh rise and planned a "one drift shot." I laid out the line and carefully estimated the distance, making sure to mend the line immediately to eliminate drag. I fell short.

"Good" I say to myself. It is better than over shooting and scaring the fish. The next cast was right on. The drift was good. He took it and the line flew off my reel. He jumped. It was a barbless hook so I had to control the line. He ran again. I brought him within a leader of my net, which was on too short a cord. I pulled and the eye came out of the handle.

He took off again running nearly into my backing. I fumbled with the net while trying manage this fish. To free my hand for reeling, I stuck it in my waders.

I brought him in again and he ran again. Amazing strength these wild fish have. This section of the Delaware is never stocked, all natural fish and this one was big.

On the next attempt I managed to get the net on him. He was beautiful. A large brown with extraordinary colors and markings. I stood there marveling at him as I tried to figure out how to estimate his size. I put my rod down in the shallow water and measured him on the net using my forceps to scratch a mark on the handle. I wish Jerry had come up to see this guy. The fly came out easily and I held him gently in the flow as he regained his bearings. After a few moments he took off like a shot.

I stuck the net back in my waders and picked my rod up out of the river, not really thinking about the fact that it could have been taken downstream. I checked the line and fly. As I tugged, the fly came off in my hand. How close I was to losing that magnificent fish.

I looked in my box to see if I had another fly like it since this one was a bit chewed up. I found none. Strange, since I never buy one fly. I looked again and then figured there must be more in the tackle bag, back in the cabin.

Part of me wanted to rush back to camp to tell my story, somewhat motivated by the cold rain and on coming darkness. Instead I tied the fly on and waited for another rise. The river was quiet. I worked my way slowly downstream when a splash on the opposite bank caught my attention. I waited and he rose again. I laid out the line and made the first cast right on the mark. He took it and I was off to the races again, barely recovered from the last one. He ran the reel again and again: three times and a jump. I got the net out once the leader was at the tip and raised the rod to bring him in, a strong rainbow this time. Not quite as large but just as beautiful. I made a second mark on my net and released him. It was still raining, cold and almost 7. I headed back to camp.

After telling my tale we took the measure of the marks on my net -19 inches for the brown and 16 for the rainbow. Jerry identified the fly as a Cornuda. I still could not find any more.

I was wracking my brain on where it came from when I remembered that I received a selection of flies from TU for a donation I made and there was one of each in the set. This was one of them.

Tom

Letters to Mack

Chapter Two

April Trout

2006

Mack,

We got up there too late to fish Thursday but it was a nice ride. The chalkboard in town said the river was at 48 degrees, a little cold for good trout action.

When we checked into the motel, the same red painted, green roofed 1950's place we usually stay at, the daughter-in-law was at the desk. She was explaining to the guys ahead of us how her father-in-law passed away last week.

> "It was sudden, although he did cough all the time. He was only 61."

The motel was bought a few years ago by this family and the father ran the operation while everyone pitched in. They kept it clean and in operating condition as well as tried to make some improvements, but obviously not able to invest too much. The complimentary morning coffee and donuts were always worthwhile.

As she gave us our key, her young daughter came out of the attached house crying. She explained how much her little girl missed her grandpa.

We went to dinner at the Italian restaurant since the place across the street finally bit the bullet after three years of great food at New York City prices in a town not used to them.

In the morning we went to the fly shops to hear the gossip on how the fishing was and what was working. The good news was that there were good late day hatches and the bad news - there were no fish:

> "Now we know there ARE fish, they just are not cooperating" the proprietor quickly added.

We bought a few flies, emergers and cripples, and I restocked my streamer wallet.

Next stop was the Covered Bridge Pool, the only open water on the upper Beaverkill. A beautiful spot with a NYS campsite along the river which was not open yet. One wonders why it doesn't open in conjunction with the trout season since trout fishermen are about all it attracts.

Dad used to bring us up here to camp and play in the freezing cold mountain stream while he attempted to catch trout.

Jerry and I drifted some nymphs through the pool where he caught a huge rainbow when he first began fishing, in the early 50's. There were some suckers on the bottom but no trout to be seen. We took a look further downstream. They must be getting ready to open as the camp sites were stocked with picnic tables and some firewood.

Next we headed upstream to visit the Beaverkill Valley Inn, a hotel and restaurant that we used to stay at when they had access to 3 miles of the private waters. Now they just have 1 mile that runs from their property up to Joan Wulff's school. The place looked exactly the same, although the rates had gone up. It would be a nice place to stay except the 3 delicious meals they serve tempt you into less fishing. We took a brochure and headed for the Willowemoc.

There is a spot about 2 miles up from Livingston Manor that we like, off DeBruce Road. It has a long, flat upstream stretch with reasonably deep pools on both banks as well as two runs created by some islands downstream. The one to the left, when looking downstream, is a beautiful forested run for about a quarter mile and on the right is a deeper, more channeled one that borders a recently built mansion with acres of tended lawn, two ponds and who knows what other luxuries. I am not sure if it is a home, a resort or a club. I like the left better.

Jerry likes to walk up the highway to the head of the pool and I usually start right by the parking area. There is a log diversion there that creates a deep pool and undercut bank. I dapped my streamer in the flow before getting into the stream and was surprised by an immediate hit. I worked it and got a second hit but struck so hard I ripped the fly off the line. After the required expletive, I put on another Black Nosed Dace and managed another hit, but no hook up. I waited and again a hit with no hook up. Then again, same routine. I finally left him to his peace but planned on coming back. We fished until almost 3:30 and caught nothing. Tried my friend again, was hit and failed to hook up. We headed for Barnhart's Pool.

Jerry reasoned that there are more hatches on the Beaverkill. I countered with the same hatch occurs here, you just have to wait for it.

His is a self-fulfilling prophecy as we leave and arrive when all the hatches occur, or so I believe. At Barnhart's we met another fellow who was less than friendly as we walked in. We headed upstream and worked our way down. Plenty of room, plenty of flies, no fish. On the way out our friend said he hooked two, but landed none, on a Hendrickson cripple. He immediately clarified that he really only hooked one, the other was a snag. His credibility rose a bit. We chatted. He showed me a photo of an Alaskan rainbow which must have measured 18 inches, around its girth.

We headed for the motel and cleaned up for dinner. It was filling up. Lots of spin fishermen in camo-colored gear with their hunting licenses still hanging from the back of their jackets. Unusual for the rivers up here, most use fly rods.

A fellow was walking by, having come from the office, and acknowledged us with a hello. I returned the gesture and he stopped and began to engage. He had reddish hair which had gone mostly gray and was thinning. He swept it over in a helmet-like fashion. He soon got my name and began to talk of his Scottish lineage inferring that the Hatfield – McCoy's of Appalachia fame were of such heritage and so must I be. I thought it strange since in fact I do have a Scottish blood line and made the mistake of continuing the conversation.

He went on about some clan or group of clans along the border. I asked if it was the Kentucky border and he said emphatically:

"No, the Scottish border."

How we got there I don't know, but next we are into Scottish history and the King and Queen and a book he read and that I need to read called *The Steel Helmet*. Perhaps that is where he got the idea for his hair-doo. He moved on to the fact that he was in the maritime union and switched back to his family heritage and that they, unfortunately, have some Bush's in it.

17

I finally made my break and we had a good meal at the Riverside Inn which just opened for the season. I ate too much. Jerry commented on a recent revelation he had. No one ever leaves a Riverside meal saying:

"I should have eaten more."

Saturday was another perfect day with no clouds and bright sun. The frost was thick on the car as we drove to the diner for breakfast, the temperature in the low 40's.

The chalkboard held no hope. The river had not increased a single degree since the day before, then I noticed that it had not been updated yet. We checked the gossip in the shop. I looked at a new vest but decided I would not know what to do with the old one which is my original. I couldn't throw it out, so I passed, promising myself to sew up the tears and maybe wash it.

I saw the son of the motel owner as we packed up and prepared to check out. I told him I was sorry for his loss. I considered sharing with him how my father died at 49 but didn't. As I was walking away he said something. I turned as I did not understand. He repeated:

"You are about his age and you are fishing still."

I nodded and again went to tell him more, but didn't.

I convinced Jerry that we should go to the Willowemoc again and, this time, stay until the hatch occurs. He agreed and we assumed the same positions. I tried my fish again and he came out again and hit the fly again and did not take it. Smartest fish I have ever met.

I wandered down through the forest on the left trying every likely spot. I came back and we had some lunch out of the cooler. I again pitched my theory of waiting for the hatch. We both went upstream and sat on the bank for an hour or more.

As I rearranged my flies, checked my leader and added a new tippet, I thought how fortunate I am to have entered a stage of my life where sitting quietly, waiting for a potential event, is possible. How difficult it would be to have someone not schooled in trout or patience to do this. I could not have done it years ago. When I teach my grandchildren to fish, I hope they are able to accept this part of it, waiting as the deer hunter waits in his stand.

About 3 O'clock there was a rise just across the stream near where I have taken nice fish before. I worked my way over and made a few casts but he was non-responsive. Jerry worked his way downstream and I followed. We were both near defeated.

One more attempt at my fish, this time with a Black Wooly-bugger. He came out, took a look and didn't even bother to hit it. We got in the car.

We agreed to stop at the Rhododendron Pool on the way home. It is just south of Roscoe, behind a highway rest stop on Route 17. It is one of the most picturesque pools on the river and has the advantage of a rest room and picnic table to use before getting on the road. Two guys were leaving as we headed for the stream. Three others were at the head. Jerry went below the swimming hole which was unusual for him. He almost always goes upstream here. I got in just above the hole and waited for some indication of a fish, but saw none. I put on a big stonefly, not that the fish were taking them, but I needed a change. Jerry was fishing the Hendrickson emerger. There were some flies on the water, but mostly caddis.

Next I tried a nymph and then a streamer, watching Jerry casting away with his emerger below me. A fellow came by and said hello. We talked of how slow the fishing was and then I heard the shriek:

"I got one."

It was Jerry and he did indeed. His rod, a new Sage he just bought to replace the Loomis he gave his daughter when we were in New Mexico last summer, was well bent and his old Hardy was singing as the line ran off.

I shouted my congratulations and immediately felt better. I waited for him to net it and show me, but the fish kept running.

"It's a big one."

This is code for me to head toward him to take a photo. I always have a disposable camera with me but he said he had his so I didn't pick one up at the store earlier. As I arrived the fish was making yet another run. He had his net out but could not get the fish near it. I had to back off to make certain it didn't use me to break off.

I hesitated asking if he wanted me to net it for him, as the guides often do when we fish with them. I decided to leave him to his own victory. More running and finally a scoop of the net ended the fight. Almost breathless with excitement, he said it was the biggest fish he had ever caught in this hole. He immediately amended it to the biggest in the Catskills. I asked for his camera and he said:

"It's in the car."

We held the fish against his rod and made a mental mark that it was 2 inches longer than the writing at the base – I thought 22 to 23 inches to be sure, with a big head and strong girth, a big fish. He thought out loud of taking him home. This was a wild fish. He let him swim away.

I called him the next morning at home to tell him of a show on TV about fly fishing for striped bass on the North Fork, something he and I are scheduled to do in a few weeks. He said it was 20.5 inches.

"Hell, make it 21" I said.

Tom

Letters to Mack

Chapter Three

May Trout

2006

Mack,

Trip 1

The West Branch Angler trip is our annual week of fishing. We arrived the Monday after Mother's Day. In fact we used to leave on Mother's Day afternoon, if you can believe that. Our wives are indeed very giving where our fishing is concerned. Over the last few years we have gone later in the month, but with my grandson's birthday party on Saturday this year, we were able to book the original week.

The itinerary was for Manny and I to meet Moe and Jerry up there. We scheduled a float trip for Tuesday. The place was so busy that we could only get one guide. We let Moe and Manny go with the guide and I rowed a second boat with Jerry behind them. The guide was named Jan. He was not too happy that a second pair was going to bird dog him down the river even though we let him know that we would be showing our gratitude.

We came through the Stilesville area okay but endured some jeers from fisherman when we hugged the far bank rather than going behind them as is the courteous way to pass. I was intending to go behind but followed Jan's route. Jerry and I kept our distance and fished the river from the weir to below Deposit, mostly out of sight of the trio. We stopped and fished the pools above and below town managing not to catch a bunch of rising fish, including some that were tailing like bone fish. They must have been taking something that was in the process of emerging but not yet on the surface.

As we headed further downstream we came to what I call the Willow Pool and heard Moe calling to us. He and Jan were up on a well maintained lawn having lunch at a picnic table. They told us Manny had walked upstream. We both said nothing and went on about our lunch. They embellished the story and expressed concern that Manny is lost upstream. I just said:

"He will find his way."

They were perplexed at our lack of concern. I know Manny a long time and he knows how to handle himself. Finally they had to tell us that he fell in and got soaked.

Luckily the home owner, (at whose table they were eating), was kind enough to drive him back to camp.

We finished our lunch and the guide shared a brownie with us as well as a few off color jokes. He then gave us some advice on fishing this particular hole. It was at the bend by the Willow and there were multiple erratic rises in the shallow riffle.

I was throwing a Hendrickson which seemed to be the fly of choice. After an extended time with no takers, I switched to a smaller Hendrickson and concentrated on one fish among all the rises. A 17 inch beauty resulted. Jan got out of the boat, netted and released him, although I did not ask him to – or want the help. I buried the thoughts, thanked him, and let it go.

Moe, fishing from the boat just below us, caught two nice fish. Jerry was batting zero so far.

The rest of the float was uneventful, although we did see enough rising fish to keep our interest. Moe and Jan went in ahead of us and so the next day we left his gratuity at the office and Manny also left a gift certificate for the fellow that drove him. We were generous, we thought.

Moe had to leave early. The next day, the three of us were fishing the riffle downstream of our cabin. Manny caught a big brown on a large mahogany spinner. The rest of the week was good with more feisty stream bred trout, but it was not productive for Jerry who, for whatever reason, caught only one small brown.

Trip 2

At the club banquet in early April, Jerry and I bid on and won two trips. The first was a day of salt water fly fishing for striped bass with Rob Thompson out of Greenport, (www.captainrobthompson.com). We fished Hallock Bay in Orient and caught 10 fish between us, the largest being a 28 inch, 6.5 pound striper. It was a great experience and something I'd certainly do again.

Trip 3

The other trip was a two night stay at the Delaware River Club, Al Caucci's place on the West Branch in Starlight, PA. It is a dated motel unit which has been decently maintained across from a great pool filled with fish, as well as an amazing chef, Fabio. He cooks anything you want for breakfast and has a one-sitting dinner at 9 PM which is the best food in the Catskills. It is served family style with Fabio doing all of the work from setting the table to cooking, serving and cleaning up.

Jerry, Moe, Mickey and I had stayed there about 16 years ago and taken their course on fishing the West Branch. It was the scene of the infamous loop clipping. We had two guides: Jim, a tall lanky fellow who was a good fisherman and a nice guy. (He passed away a few years ago, unexpectedly, at a young age.) The other guy was Jean, an obnoxious know it all. They were showing us how to make a leader connection to the fly line with Krazy Glue which was seamless and easily passed through the guides, not that you ever want to have your leader in the guides, at least not with a fish on.

Moe had spent hours affixing a loop to which he attached his leader before the trip. Jean, without asking, took Moe's line and clipped off the loop, insisting that his way is better. Moe was furious and the guy did not even offer to tie one back on. He just insisted that his way was better and you'd have to be an idiot to want it any other way. We all pretty much had our fill of Jean and his know-it-all-ness. It so happens that I prefer a loop for quick leader changes as do a lot of folks.

Anyway, this was years ago and we wanted to take advantage of what we thought was a great bargain. More importantly we wanted access to their Home Pool, so off we went.

Moe couldn't make it nor could Manny. Jerry called Mickey who was glad to be invited and accepted right away. We had not seen him since the golf bug bit him a number of years ago. We met at the Roscoe Diner, (where else?), and headed up to Deposit as we had rented a drift boat for the day.

We put in at the weir and didn't get to the first bridge when I realized the boat was flooding. I had Mickey check the plugs and sure enough they were loose. We pulled over and Mickey bailed us out using a small cooler. I later wondered if the lodge just forgot to tighten them or if

some mischief was done. As we passed through
Stilesville and on to Deposit, we went behind wading
fishermen, as we should.

There were no rises and few bugs on the water as we
worked to get Mickey a fish after his long hiatus. By lunch
time we were at Danager's Pool (aka the willow tree) and
who was there but Jan, the guide, with two new charges.
We said hello and he passed a comment about going
swimming. We chuckled. Jerry suggested we pull over
and use the picnic table. I felt awkward walking on
someone's property without permission and asked Jan if
he thought the owner would mind. He hesitated and
indicated it would not be a good idea.

Now we had met the owner a few times since Manny's
swim. He was fishing the river one day when we came by
on foot and we chatted. We also saw him up at the fly
shop. Manny had a good conversation with him about his
fabricating business which he could relate to. We were
pretty sure he would not mind our intrusion. However, we
backed off and set the boat on the bank downstream to
have our lunch. Then Jan and company went to the table.
Hmmm.

We fished the next day on foot, covering a few pools up
and downstream as well as the Home Pool, with little luck.

At the cocktail hour we compared notes with about 20
other guests to find that no one had a good day. Just to
prove to his grumbling guests that it could be done,

Caucci went out right before dinner and caught a nice rainbow in the Home Pool. Very cool.

Dinner was a five course affair with hot and cold appetizers, salad, soup and a main course followed by dessert, all hosted graciously by Al and his lovely wife. We got to meet fellow fishers from all walks of life. Fishing aside, the food, the host, and our dining companions made for a great experience that I would do again.

Tom

Letters to Mack

Chapter Four

June Trout

2006

Mack,

The trip this refers to is the one I took with the guys from the club.

It is an annual event I had never gone to before, partly because I have only recently become active in the organization and part because by the second week in June I had usually been upstate for at least 10 days and never wanted to push it too far with the Mrs.

This year Jerry said he was interested and so we signed up. As it turned out, he had to cancel due to a family obligation which took him out west. He had to settle for a day fishing the Rockies instead.

I drew Joe as a room-mate and we decided to drive up together. He was nice enough to come all the way up to the Neck to pick me up. We hit it off right away. He asked if I'd like to fish the Neversink on the way up. He had family from upstate that knew the river, Cousin Eddie. We arranged to meet him at exit 107 by Holiday Mountain at 9 AM.

I had not fished the Neversink in many years and was not familiar with the public access points. I was excited to meet Eddie who told Joe he had a secret spot. It turned out to be a parking lot across from a ski shop just outside the gates of the park and in sight of Route 17, right under our noses all these years. We have driven by it a hundred times, always checking the water level in the river as we passed at 65 mph.

Eddie suggested we start in the middle of the run and try caddis. Joe immediately caught a fish. I headed downstream to give everyone some room. There were rises up and down the river. The water was a little discolored from the recent rains but wadable. I caught a trout or two on a small Blue Wing Olive.

Later we worked our way upstream and into the flat water just below the bridge. Again there were small fish rising all over, although not all that often. I managed a few more on the BWO. Joe got into a strong fish downstream of me, I'd guess a full 15 inches.

At noon, we gathered at the car to say good bye to Eddie
and head up to the Riverside Lodge in Horton where we
rent out all the rooms for the weekend. Dinner was to be at
5 so we had some time to try another spot after we
checked in.

We decided to fish the water behind the lodge. Joe went to
the Sunoco Pool and I headed downstream, below the
riffle, to the next piece of smooth water. This is the no kill
section so I figured there should be fish throughout and
wanted to avoid the crowd (and spectators) upstream. It
was rough walking in the stream as the rocks were odd
sizes and not well organized. I almost dunked myself so I
headed to shore to walk the rest of the way down.

I tried to hit the pockets and pillows as best I could but
with no success. I set up across from the pool on the far
side and just waited, as I often do, watching for some sign
before expending the energy to cast. It was a long wait.

I tied on the Usual, a fly I found through Fran Betters up
on the West Branch of the Ausable. Being a traditional dry
fly guy, I was surprised to hear that so many guys in the
group used it down here. I made a few blind casts and
started to work my way upstream with the goal of getting
to the lodge in time for dinner.

Since this was my first trip with the group I was confused
as to why they wanted us off the stream at 5 PM. Jerry and
I usually have lunch and fish until dark. I am trying to be
open to new ideas and new friends, so didn't ask the
question. I did review with myself the possibility that if

the fish began to rise I just might be late for my first meal with my new room-mate.

The fish did not materialize and it looked as if I would be on time when I thought I saw a flash to my fly. I stopped, waited and re-cast. A nice fish came up and took a good look, then refused. I made a fly change and tried again, and again, but he was either gone or resolved not to take my fly.

Dinner was a BBQ with a ton of food. We all ate too much and I then asked the ridiculous question:

"What are we going to do after dinner?"

I somehow figured there was a meeting or ceremony or entertainment. I can be so stupid sometimes. Joe looked at me in disbelief and said:

"Fish."

Each set of roomies went off to the pool of their choice. Joe and I went upstream and settled for Barnhart's as Peter and Boyd were already at Hendrickson's.

I saw some rises at the head of the pool and there were bugs on the water but, as I recall, neither of us connected. They call this week, the second in June, Bug Week since there is so much going on. BWO as always, given the lousy weather. Grey Foxes, Sulfurs, Isonychias, March Browns, Green and Brown Drakes with the possibility of spinners from all of them. We headed back at near dark and passed Boyd's car still on the side of the road. I half wanted to stop but figured they were probably in the process of coming out.

We sat on the porch and compared notes as the rain continued. No one did particularly well although Jeff got into a good one and Jay did well on the Willow just above the Junction. Darkness fell and we were discussing the mayflies coming to the light bulb or caught in the spider webs when Peter and Boyd appeared. After some prodding, Peter admitted to ten fish. Ten Fish. I had heard he was a good fisherman, but ten fish on a pool Jerry and I usually pass up and at a time when most of us weren't doing even one? I asked:

"On what?"

"Henryville Special."

"A caddis?"

I didn't even see one and we were only about 200 yards upstream. I mentally checked my box and noted where the Henryville's were for tomorrow.

The evening ended with some guitar, harmonica and singing which was fun although the group dwindled down to about 5 by the time they came to the audience participation part. Peter's version of the Hank Snow/Johnny Cash song re-named "I've Fished Everywhere Man" was fun, even for a tune-less person such as me.

I was up early as is my way, dressed and was heading to the Sunoco for my morning coffee when I ran into Tony and George. They had the same plan and Tony offered to give me a lift. We had to wait until 6 AM on the nose for the door to open but were pleased to see two steaming pots of fresh java waiting for us. We yakked a bit as we prepared our brews. They were heading upstream to try their luck. I wished them well and walked back to the lodge to see if Joe was up to some early morning fishing.

He was just rolling over so I put on my gear and walked back to the path behind the Sunoco. As I was passing the pumps it occurred to me that I walked out without paying for my coffee. I felt like a jerk but went in to ante up. The lady laughed and said not to worry, my friends had taken care of it.

When I got to the pool, Scott, Eddie and another fellow were in the water. Scott had taken a few fish and showed me what was working for him. I put on a mahogany spinner and hit a nice fish.

Breakfast was amazing. The food just kept coming and we again ate too much. Pete brought hats to sell and we all discussed our plans for the day as we passed the French toast. Joe and I went to town and then up the Willow. When we arrived there were three cars already there, leaving only one spot for us to park, in the mud. Joe maneuvered us in without incident. I had promised to show him my trained fish but he was not cooperating this day.

Three fellows from our group were in position just upstream of the parking lot. Joe took the spot above them, below the trailer home, and I went up to the riffle. I suggested he fish his way across. Although they always seem to be on the far bank under the trees, they also lay mid-stream at times. He hit a beautiful 14 inch brown, on a caddis I think, followed by an even bigger one on a Royal Coachman.

We wanted to see what Miss Trout 2006 was like so we went to Livingston Manor. We passed a caravan of cars heading up the Willow as we left.

Town was lively with music and lots of folks dressed in fish costumes. A couple was exchanging vows on stage and fun was being had by all. We had a bite to eat and headed for Cemetery Pool to see what we could do before dinner.

We had the place to ourselves which was amazing on a Saturday in June. We went up to the riffle and fished to rises without much luck, in spite of lots of bugs on the stream. A fellow came by as we were leaving. He owns the little cabin at the head of the pool. He said they were taking spinners and felt we should not leave as it was about to "snow." We tried to explain the need to join the group but he just shook his head.

Dinner was again beyond my expectations and I tried not to eat too much. The raffle was fun and Joe won a nice reel. I was thinking of the snow at Cemetery Pool and we went to pick up where we left off. Jeff, Scott and Ed decided to come along. There was only one other guy there, nymphing aggressively as there were no rises and apparently no spinners.

We all went upstream, watched and waited. Nothing. A while longer, nothing. It was getting near 8, a rise or two, but no hookups. Scott and I decided to head downstream, below where we walked in, just above the bridge.

As we were walking, we saw another fellow, (the nympher had left, untested). He had a fish on and was awkwardly chasing it downstream, apparently planning to beach it. I was thinking that I had not seen fish from this pool that called for that kind of strategy but hey, you never know.

He did land it and released him before we got close enough to bear witness. He was smiling and wet. The fish dunked him, he cheerfully told us. Jeff and Joe were trailing behind us, Ed was already further downstream.

Jeff had picked up a large Isonychia spinner when we were upstream which we all admired and this fellow mentioned that he caught his fish on a spinner. Scott continued to head down toward the bridge. I decided to try my luck in the tail of the pool. Jeff positioned himself below me and Joe just above.

The water was deep and swift, not to mention cold, as was the air. We had every stitch of clothing we brought on our bodies trying to keep warm. I even had on my "Freddie

the Freeloader" woolen gloves from the Army surplus
store with the finger tips cut off. The image of our friend
and his comment about the fish dunking him was fresh in
my mind, the fish and the dunk.

We waded out to a reasonable depth, maybe even a little
to the unreasonable side, and watched. Joe took a few
casts and we both saw a rise on the far bank. Out of range
from here but I figured I'd give it a try. Not even close. I
edged out further into the pool. The water was lapping
against my rain jacket and approaching the top of my
waders. I tried to head upstream, feeling my way and
wishing I had one of those wading staffs the other guys
carry.

I inched my way over and up hoping that I had reached the
apex of the depth. Another cast. Still out of reach. A little
further, fish and dunk going through my mind. My left
foot discovers a rock in my path. I climb up on it. It is not
flat and I have to straddle it. It gives me at least a foot of
height and I am just upstream of the rise which is only
about 12 inches off the bank. I dry my rusty spinner and
set about to cast. Short but not spooked. One more, on
target, mend, mend. He took it.

I see his head and shoulders clear the water in a splashier
than usual rise to a spinner. He is a good size. He runs out
from the bank and heads downstream. I turn him and get
him on the reel. I smile at Jeff and just as we are about to
banter about him, he heads south, my reel singing. I look
and, unbelievably, I am into my backing. I brake him by
palming but he is still going. I need to turn him. I need to

get off this rock and chase him but the probability of a dunk is too great and the conditions too cold. I am running out of line. I don't want to go to the end of the backing. In an attempt to fight him from this rock, I palm harder. Ping. It's over. What a rush.

Jeff and I did a quick reconstruction and using his emergency preparedness lingo suggests I should have had an exit plan. Right he was. I had the thought of jumping in and following him downstream but quickly ruled it out having just read about the guy who drowned at Junction Pool…plus it was cold. The hook up was the hard part, I rationalized, and the thrill. I was happy.

We headed back to the lodge to sit around the camp fire Sean built so well and watch the moon rise as the sky cleared for the first time. Talking of the Adirondacks with Jay, rehashing the day's fishing with Joe while listening to the guys reminisce about the year before when instead of cold and rain they had heat and low water.

Good company, good fishing, good food and a camp fire. What more can you ask for?

I'll be back.

Tom

Chapter Five

July Trout - A Western Journal

2006

Mack,

I had hoped to go west with Jerry again this year but when we discussed it he felt that he better plan a trip with the wife instead. I overheard some of the guys at the club meeting talking about a trip west in July; I inquired to see if there was room for one more.

Peter has been going out west each summer since 1988 and Jeff had joined him many times. This year Joe, Jay, and Pete decided to tag along as well. Tommy was going out with Peter earlier and Tony would be in the area with his wife and hoped to hook up with the group as well. I had been to the Beaverkill outing in June and enjoyed everyone's company so decided that this trip was for me.

There were some choices to make since the date range was from July 16 to July 28th. Some of them were going to fish the Green River in Utah after Montana. I wanted to go to the Green with them but would have been the odd man since they were floating, two men to a boat. I thought of fishing from the bank but then decided to stay in West Yellowstone and concentrate on those streams. I planned to arrive on the 20th and depart the 28th. Sue, as always, was very supportive.

Day 1 – July 20

I met Jeff and Joe in Salt Lake and we drove to the Slide Inn on the Madison in Montana, about 5 hours in the car with enjoyable scenery and company. We arrived in time to have burgers on the grill and fish the river which runs by the cabins that night. Jeff and Peter proved to be helpful guides to those of us who were new to the area.

The water was fast, rough, and unwadable on the main flow. Fishing was limited to the bank and quiet water nearby. We fished as a group but most of the guys had migrated over to the smaller side channel leaving Joe and I on the main river. I worked my way upstream to the rock by the beaver hut, near where the path comes in from the cabins. I was able to hook two nice rainbows by drifting a caddis imitation from the eddy behind the rock out into the flow. Joe hooked up as well. It was a good introduction to the Madison and Slide Inn.

Day 2 - July 21

Slide Inn offers a number of cabins on the river as well as camping. We gathered for breakfast of bacon and eggs in Peter's cabin with Jeff doing the cooking.

We were planning to fish two waters each day. Today was to be special as Peter was showing us some water where Artic Grayling, an endangered and scarce fish in the lower 48, were abundant. We drove on a dirt road, passed a group of teenage girls on a trail ride, and headed over the continental divide, into and out of Idaho. A badger ran across the road in front of us. He stopped by the edge of the woods to look back and snarl.

The creek runs into lakes of the same name in a meandering, high mountain meadow surrounded by willows and brush. We separated as the water was small. I fished downstream of the bridge, (which was no longer there). I had hits right away on an Adams and worked my way down, landing my first Grayling a few minutes after Jeff reported his first on the walkie-talkies we all carried.

I continued downstream catching one after another, all small. At a turn in the river where an undercut bank and willow combined to make good cover, I sunk a fly and hooked what looked like a 12 to 14 inch Grayling. He fought well and jumped but threw the hook before I could bring him to the net. Further down I came upon a very deep pool and watched as a huge fish moseyed back and forth on the bottom, apparently picking up nymphs. He had to be 20 inches plus. I sent him for cover with my

43

first attempt. I waited and watched through the crystal clear water as he eventually came back. I tried again, but to no avail. I hit a few more further downstream. The radio call came to meet for lunch. Next stop, the Madison by Three Dollar Bridge.

The Madison is a long river and has many faces. Slide Inn is downstream of Quake Lake, formed by a 7.2 earthquake in 1959. The water below the natural dam is called the Moonscape as it has not recovered from the harsh shift in geography in all these years. Then Slide Inn followed by Raynold's Pass. Further down, Three Dollar Bridge and then Mile Marker 13 make up the near at hand hot spots.

The Bridge is a favorite and we went there for the night, and I mean night as we didn't come off the river until after 10 PM. The water upstream is divided into three distinct areas. On the near side of the bank are a lot of large boulders and pocket water. On the far side there is some bank fishing into the main flow with some boulders and pockets as well. But the location of choice, at least for us, was the gravel bar and islands mid-stream.

At the upper end of the gravel bar you could fish the main flow where Tommy, Jeff and Peter all connected with nice fish. I tried the pocket water and had fish rising to my fly, but only once. To get them to come up after a refusal meant putting on a new fly. I did not manage a hook up this night but thoroughly enjoyed the teasing trout of the Madison.

As it got to be 9 PM everyone moved down to the lower end of the last island where "The Rock" was. We had seen video of this spot the year before at a club meeting. It was amazing how many fish were coming up, jumping and sticking their heads out of the water behind the protection of this large rock in the middle of the main flow, its force keeping normal people from wanting to wade out to fish it. Peter had somehow figured out how to get out far enough, reaching over the rushing water, to land a fly in the back wash of the rock. He demonstrated by promptly getting a fish on. Jeff was next and likewise connected, then Tommy and Joe, who was unsuccessful. I tried it but did not connect either. We had a good first day together and were all exhausted as we marched out with our head lamps on looking like the seven dwarfs coming home from the mine.

Day 3 – July 22

After a good breakfast of Peter's home-made French Toast we packed up and left Slide Inn for the Lazy G in West Yellowstone, (and dropped Tommy off at the airport). It is a motel run by Janice who has been taking care of Peter and company for years. She has clean rooms, coffee in the morning and coolers with ice, all included at a very reasonable rate, plus, she always has a smile on her face. We met up with Jay and Pete who arrived the day before. Once checked in we went to Blue Ribbon Flies to renew acquaintances with the owner, Craig Mathews, and to stock up on whatever flies we didn't get the first day at Henry's Fork Anglers, where we bought our licenses.

First stop was Grayling Creek. Now this may be a little confusing but this creek does not have any Grayling. At least not enough that any of us could hope to catch one. It does have a nice population of rainbows, cutts and browns. It is a beautiful little stream running along the road for a few miles with a variety of water. We again split up, each taking a mile marker and either working up or downstream. It was truly fun water with mostly small and accessible fish that responded to Royal Wulff and Adams dry flies. It is also in a remote and wild location in spite of the road being only a few yards away. It is at the foot of the big burn of 1988 and had habitat suited to all the critters of the Park, including bears. I took some time to wander off into the meadow but did not see any foot prints or, for that matter, any bears. At the appointed hour we all walked out to the road and the guy with the car came by and picked us up. I showed them a large bone I had come across. Someone commented that it was too short for an elk and too fat for a deer… could it have been from a bear? More likely a buffalo.

Our next stop was the Gallatin. We pulled off by the Black Butte Ranch. Jay, Pete and I went downstream while the others went up to the bridge. I crossed to the other side and worked my way down, running into some very thick willows and brush. When out in this country you are always mindful that it is possible to run into the local wildlife, anything from a snake to a bear. It makes the day that much more exciting. I picked up a few nice browns working my way down to a long pool, all on dries. Jay and Pete were already there waiting for the hatch.

I had a few nice fish while we waited. Pete was working a fish next to the bank that kept rising throughout the day and into the evening but was not to be caught. Jay had a nice rainbow. Then we were blessed with a spinner fall that was so thick Jay was covered in them. A Rusty Spinner was the fly to use. I picked up a few more fish before the agreed to quitting time. We headed out across the meadow in the dark. It was a good walk back to the car and a little scary. We were all exhausted.

Day 4 – July 23

Peter introduced his word of the day game. He had selected obscure words and printed them out on sheets of paper. Each day he posted it in the window of his room and we were all to try to figure it out over breakfast. It was the teacher in him coming out but it was also good fun.

We took a morning to get some things done in town like shopping, re-provisioning and laundry. We visited every fly shop in town and a few souvenir shops too. There is a lot of water to fish out here and I love visiting new water, but the group voted to head for the Madison and Three Dollar Bridge again. I worked the downstream pockets this time with Jeff and Joe, both of whom had several nice fish on. I had hits and refusals.

We moved to Mile Marker 13 for the evening, parking at the most downstream end of the dirt road. We fished the gravel bar where Joe hooked a very nice rainbow, as did Peter.

The Madison had not yielded to me yet, except for that first night at Slide Inn.

Day 4 – July 24

Yellowstone Park was on the agenda for today. We took our time stopping, like all the other tourists, to see the animals, hot springs and water falls. The fires of 1988 are still very much in evidence. They burned 37% of the 2+ million acre park. New growth is all over and the burned trees are slowly falling to the ground. Those that know say that the burn has increased the number of animals in the park and enriched the soil. The policy is to allow burns to occur naturally and let the forest recover naturally, as it has for millions of years. This is truly a wild place.

That evening we fished the Yellowstone River at Nez Perce, (aka Buffalo Ford), a few miles downstream of Fishing Bridge. The area was well named. As we were fishing we heard some snorts and growls and over the rise came a buffalo and then another, followed by a small herd. The growling continued until one of them was separated from the group and wandered upstream on his own, walking across from us on the far bank. Then another was cut out of the pack. He decided to cross the river – right where Jay and Pete were in the water.

It proved to be a tough day on the Yellowstone with only Peter connecting. He landed a large cutthroat on a small dry fly. We all tried to replicate his fly and method but no more hookups even though we fished until the dark was upon us. As we packed up for the Lazy G, the stars came out in all their glory. What a beautiful place to be.

Driving out in the pitch black of night was another thing. With all the animals we had passed on the way in, I kept thinking we were going to careen into a buffalo for sure.

Day 5 - July 25

This was the last day for Jeff, Joe, Jay and Pete as they were heading down to Utah to fish the Green River tomorrow. We decided to fish Cabin Creek, a section of the Madison which is in-between Hebgen and Quake Lakes.

The area was originally flooded when the earthquake dammed the river but each year the water recedes a little, opening more of this section to fishing. It is in a beautiful valley and filled with trout and whitefish. I chose to fish upstream in the pockets along the bank. I passed a few collapsed cabins, hence the name, and caught a good amount of small energetic trout.

Walking the bank I scared a few small snakes in the grass. I came across one that was struggling to carry a frog he had in his mouth into the grass where he could take his time and enjoy his meal.

I moved downstream to join the others as a huge thunder storm was moving up the valley. We could hear the rumbles and see the clouds but the rain was beyond our vision, surrounded by steep mountain sides as we were. We made it back to the cars just as the skies opened up.

We moved downstream to Three Dollar where you could see for hundreds of miles across the Madison Valley. What an awesome sight. It was clear that the storm had already passed this area. We fished the pockets and that evening we split up with Jay, Pete and I going to the Henry's Fork by the Railroad Ranch where they had fished with success earlier in the week. New water for me.

The Henry's Fork has been a place I wanted to fish ever since reading of Hemingway and his son fishing it. It is a famous flow in Idaho and part of the Snake River. Its Box Canyon is said to hold huge trout and its share of rattle snakes. The Ranch was donated by the Harriman's, same as Harriman Park in New York. Peter had warned that it was tough fishing but I needed to see it. Jay and Pete had stayed at the Trout Hunter on its banks and took me there for a good dinner of Mom's Meatloaf. We saw a young moose on the road in Last Chance as we drove down.

It is a big, wide river with a strong flow although fairly shallow at about 3 feet. I looked for structure but there is very little. Pete and Jay set up just off the pier by the parking and I moved downstream. They had rising fish but no takers. I saw one or two sporadic rises and otherwise had to blind cast to a featureless river.

I watched two other fishermen who were downstream of me to see what their technique was. They stood on the bank and watched. When a rise occurred they moved out and fished to it, moving back to their observation post afterwards. Made sense given the size of the water but it was getting dark and the bank by me was covered with willows so thick I would have needed a machete to get through them. I went back to where the others were and took a few futile casts at their risers before we headed for home. I had not had my fill of the Henry's Fork.

Day 6 – July 26

We saw off the Green River gang with hugs and shakes, then Peter and I discussed what we wanted to do for the day. As we were talking Tony walked up. He was on vacation with his wife and arrived the night before. We invited them to breakfast and he fished with us the next two days while his wife saw the sights.

Peter had promised to fish the Henry's Fork with me so that is where we headed. We went to the dam and fished the tail waters which were a beautiful bluish green color. We worked the water hard but besides a hit on a nymph, none of us scored. Drift boats came by along with kayaks to work the Box Canyon below us and one of them hooked a nice fish just out of reach of my wading position.

We moved to the Madison. Tony wanted to fish Mile Marker 13 but when we assessed the water it was over the gravel bar due to agricultural releases from the dam. We moved to Three Dollar (again). Tony and I fished the downstream pockets while Peter took a nap.

I caught a few small fish and then came upon three rising fish in the mid-stream wake of a boulder. I quietly moved into position, keeping in mind how these fish only give you one refusal. I put on a likely pattern and they didn't refuse it, they ignored it, continuing to rise. I lowered my eye to the water trying to determine what it was they were taking but could not see anything. It must have been just below the surface.

I switched to emerger patterns but received a similar response. I then thought I may be at a disadvantage being downstream of them. I recalled the San Juan strategy of presenting the fly first, counter to normal eastern tactics. I moved up and behind a boulder and flipped them my offering. Nothing. Again and again I tied on a different fly and flipped it, gently, not disturbing the water or dragging. Nothing.

I put on a # 16 dry Epeorius, even though there were none on the water that I could see, and finally – I got a refusal. That would be the best I could do on these fish. I moved to the bank, had some trail mix and water, and went upstream to join the others.

Tony and Peter were on the gravel bar above the bridge we had fished before. It was almost 9 PM and Peter suggested we try "The Rock" as the fish were predictably rising. I had tried and failed the second night and was not all that enthusiastic about standing in that treacherous torrent. Then I thought: all the other guys had success at The Rock so I have to do it.

Peter gave me a large Usual with a pink body like the bubblegum fly. The bubblegum pattern has proven successful on this river time and time again, even though it resembles absolutely nothing natural.

As we moved into position, I could see the heads and sometimes the whole bodies of the fish coming up, aggressively taking whatever was on the water. Peter went first to demonstrate the technique once more. I watched. He hooked up with a nice fish in a few casts. The main concern was to get the fly and the fly line over the rapid that was coming off of The Rock, which was the size of a wave at Gilgo Beach on a good day. Peter is a tall guy with long arms and a 9 foot rod. He was able to do this fairly naturally. I had the same size rod but everything else was smaller and with my shoulder surgery, the extension on the right arm is limited in reach and strength.

I made my cast and managed to achieve the goal - a few feet of drift behind The Rock before the force of the water pulled it out. I retrieved and cast again. A few more casts and I was into a nice fish that was running, jumping, and trying to throw the hook. My instinct was to tighten the line but Peter insisted that I just back myself out of the current and get on the gravel bar before worrying about the fish. I did as he said and after a good fight landed a nice fish. A rainbow. I released him and he kicked right away, even after the fight and the photo. No need to revive him. Strong fish. I went back and hooked another who later freed himself. Then another that I landed. The last one ran into the backing and fought such that I would have expected a monster. He was a modest fish with a lot of heart. I thanked Peter for the coaching and we headed back in the dark. The Madison had finally yielded to my efforts.

Day 7 – July 27

Our last day in Montana. We did some shopping and then headed for Grayling Creek as it is also one of Tony's favorites. I got in at mile marker 13.5 and fished upstream a few hundred yards. It was as beautiful as the section below mile-marker 12 where I fished the first time, although easier to wade as there was more gravel. I hit numerous small trout on Adams and Royal Wulffs when I came across a log by the bank that just had to hold fish. Neither fly elicited a response. There were just too many fish in the stream for that to be the case so I assumed whatever was in there had a more sophisticated palate. I tied on a caddis and floated it over the exact same spot. Wham. A nice rainbow of good size.

Next we headed for the Gallatin and drove past Black Butte to a place further downstream where none of us had fished before. I went up, Tony down and Peter took the middle stretch. It was fast moving and lots of riffles, runs, and small pools. I found a side channel and fished it from bottom to top getting one rise. I saw a big splash right next to the bank, across from me, and assumed it was to a grasshopper. I tied one on but no reaction. Then I put on a small stimulator and worked it all along that bank. It sunk in the current and I let it continue downstream when I felt the tug-tug-tug I had been hoping for. A good size rainbow was the result.

We met at the appointed hour and I assumed we were going to head for one more stretch but we headed for Eino's instead. The décor is that of a rowdy bar but there were magnificent views of the entire valley and West Yellowstone. They had all the doors open but there were no flies in the place. We noticed bags of water hanging over each door. This is what keeps the flies out. Go figure.

We sat on the porch talking while we digested our meal. Peter called Jeff to see how they made out on the Green. It was a long trip but they had a good day. Pete caught a record 12 fish which made us all feel good. Full of good food and tired from the week of marathon fishing, we decided not to fish the evening. We headed back to town and packed up for tomorrow's return trip.

It was a great trip with fish, flora, fauna and friendship. I am already thinking about doing it again next year. Maybe Jackson Hole? Maybe Slough Creek or the Lamar?

Tom

Letters to Mack

Chapter Six

Putnam Pond

2006

Mack,

Upstate was nice. I had three camp grounds picked out and figured I would go to each and check them before deciding where to stay. Paradox Lake was first. Nice but the lake was big and somewhat developed. Next I went to a place called Putnam Pond, east of the Northway at exit 28, about 10 miles down Rt. 74 and then 3.5 miles into the mountains. These are not the high peaks I usually go to but rather the foot hills of the Adirondacks, just before the Lake Champlain Valley, (and the town of Ticonderoga).

It was a nice camp with each site separated from the others by at least as many trees as the site was wide. Fairly quiet, although there were two families across from one another that were constantly shouting back and forth. The pond is a lake by Long Island standards, beautiful and undeveloped. I guess about 50 acres or more. Deep enough so you couldn't see bottom. It also had a stream coming out of it which was small, tumbling over rocks and around boulders with a thick canopy to keep it cool.

I set up camp and went fly fishing on the stream catching a few native brook trout in the 6 - 7 inch range. I was using the 3 weight, 6 foot bamboo I got in April. It is a composite of rod parts refitted to work together. It has fine action and is very light. I was pulling line through the tip and it snapped on me, right at the ferrule, the wood apparently rotten. It happens, looked repairable and I didn't get upset, but there were still fish rising. I took the tip section, tied a leader to it, and continued to fish - and catch.

The Coleman stove and lantern, which had not been used in years, fired right up. I had my standard first night camp dinner of hamburger and beans, sat and watched the camp fire and slept pretty well.

The next morning I rented a canoe and paddled around the pond. It is quiet and picturesque with lily pads, some interesting rock formations and islands. I had a rod and threw a few casts. Caught a small yellow perch and a sunny but really enjoyed the gliding canoe and the view more.

After lunch I hiked to a back woods brook trout pond about 2 miles in, called Rock Pond. Nice walk with some elevation but not too hard. Good thing because I am not in the best of shape after skipping workouts all spring. The pond was beautiful with rock out croppings all around and some islands, but it was crowded. There was a lean-to which was occupied, at least three groups in tents and two more came by while I was standing there. The water was high according to one of the hikers. He had to cross through the water in a spot where a path had been the last time he was here.

I packed a small spinning rod and flipped a lure around but the access was difficult. Had I been staying over I would have waded in but didn't want to hike back with wet feet. It was 5 PM and I am sure had I stayed until 7 or 8 the brookies would have shown themselves, but I didn't want to walk back in the dark.

Had a good dinner of franks and beans and a camp fire but I was so tired I was snoozing in my chair. I snuffed out the fire and turned in early.

I woke at day break, made breakfast and broke camp. Before getting on the road, I wanted to check out another camp ground near Newcomb, about 35 miles away. I ended up making a wrong turn and just headed home.

I had not camped since the early 80s and was glad that my equipment still worked and I had not lost my touch with a one match camp fire. It was a good experience and I'd go back again.

Tom

Letters to Mack

Chapter Seven

Hannah

2006

Mack,

I drove by the cemetery today, off Old Country Road in Melville. It reminded me that it has been 4 years since we lost Hannah. I wrote this back then:

We were on the deck, Sue still in her work clothes, in facing chairs, knees touching.

Tom - "I hope she passes in peace."

Sue - "I called again. Her cousin answered the phone. I stumbled for words. She cut me off. 'She is dying and her family is with her.' Then she hung up."

Tom - "I'm going to miss her. I can't believe her strength."

She walked into my classroom, fresh from Israel. Pretty, even exotic, with her straight black hair, funny accent and a kind of nasal whine that she never lost and we grew fond of. Beauty culture was her major as we feigned being on the college preparation tract. She was more honest and insightful than we ever were. While other beauty culture girls would pour on makeup and "bouff up" their hair, she always had that pure beauty that needed no help.

I think she met him in Ryan's, a local hangout of the rougher sort. What was a nice Jewish girl doing in Ryan's?

He a Catholic and she Israeli, with parents who were religious and culturally sincere, there was no encouragement for this relationship from either side, but they had made up their minds.

We double dated in his Ford Galaxy when I first met Sue, or maybe it was the '57 Chevy. He had so many cool cars. She was sweet and embracing to Sue who was from outside our crowd. I was awful, being at the lowest and least likable years of my youth. If not for her, I may have lost Sue.

She loved people and enjoyed making them comfortable. She made no enemies that she couldn't forgive. The four of us grew closer from that point on. It was the 60's but

the quake, the great divide, the apocalypse between
generations and classmates alike, had yet to begin.

The war was heating up. Guys were signing up and getting
drafted, girls were grabbing available guys. None of us
had enough self-confidence to fill a coffee cup but no one
talked about it. We just tried to hold on to something,
anything, to make us feel a part of. Sue and I married as
did they.

We were separated by the service. I was stationed where
Sue could join me. We returned 2 years later to find
corduroy, V-neck sweaters, and penny loafers traded in for
sandals, beads, see thru blouses and ponchos. Neat hair,
well combed (it took our friend Joey at least an hour to get
his just right) was traded for straggly long locks. Beer for
wine and grass, surfing for watching a lava lamp bubble,
The Beach Boys for the White Album, Ryan's for the
Electric Circus.

Sue and I had been in a time warp. We were shocked. But
she was the same. She was the rock we could hold on to
while we tried to acclimate, which we never really did.

Sue saw her for haircuts. They spoke on the phone. We
visited with the kids in tow but gave that up as the
lifestyles of he and I began to conflict. They came for
Christmas. Both for a while, then just her. Always her.
Always with gifts. And like the movie: *Same Time Next
Year*, we walked through all the phases of the next 30+
years together. Differing at times. She never could come
to grips with the ridiculous amount of toys the boys would

get. She knew then what we are coming to know now: that this superfluous spending on material junk is mindless and harmful to all involved.

No children materialized. She held her head high. After a generous amount of time, they divorced.

Her second marriage didn't work out but gave her the love of her life, her son now 13.

Sue - "Lung? She never smoked."

Tom - "I know. Maybe it was all the hairspray?"

Surgery. Chemo. Radiation. Hair loss. Always believing that she could beat it, and for a while she did.

She never planned on being a single mom and certainly didn't deserve the grief but she took it in stride. She supported herself with her haircutting as she always had, in the shop and at home. She rented the upstairs and lived frugally. She gave her son all she could and then some.

Last June Sue called.

Sue - "Just touching base."

She told her of getting ready to take her son to Florida to visit his paternal aunt of who they were both fond. She would accompany him on the flight down and then come right back. She wasn't well.

Hannah - "On medication again. Getting treatments."

She was expanding the apartment upstairs so she could get more rent. She figured her son would benefit from the income. Always looking forward.

She called us two weeks ago and just said she was at her Mom's and getting hospice care. A small whimper of a tear, but that was it.

Sue - "Do you want us to come over?"

Hannah - "Yes."

We were part of a procession of friends, both new and old. Family, neighbors, and co-workers, even ex-in-laws crowded the Levitt house. Her brother joked that she only divorced husbands, never in-laws. We sat in the smaller of the two bedrooms. She sat up, oxygen to her nose, telling us how the new carpet is ordered and how she needs to freshen up these old bookcases. She had worked up until the week before, not about to be kept down. Her hair was her own, but frizzed. She called it "Chemo-curl" and it looked as good on her as that beautiful black hair I remember in grade school.

We talked of our motorcycle ride that burned her leg in '66. She proudly pulled up her pajamas and stuck her leg on my lap to find the scar. Then flaunted those pretty legs, not a vein to be seen, and teased me as I rubbed them. Laughing. Remembering. Telling me she always felt safe with me. Neither of us would do harm to the other.

We looked at pictures we brought of the children, grandchildren and friends, including a picture of him with his son.

Tom - "Do you want to see him?"

Immediately, without hesitation she shook her head - Yes.

Sue asked her mother, since there had been differences.

Mom - "I have no problem."

Hannah's wishes outweighed any feelings Mom had of the past.

Tom - "I'll bring him with me. I'll come too."

Mom - "That would be good."

I met him in the parking lot of the Green up the street. He was nervous. When we walked in, to his surprise, he was welcomed by all. He sat next to her at the family table which was expanded into the living room and filled with an array of partially eaten food.

They laughed and reminisced. Typical of her, she got in a few instructions on how to be a good father. Cautioned him that his children should not do what we did.

Hannah - "Are they good students? Help them with their homework. Stay close to them."

She was leaving to do her banking, to put things in order, oxygen bottle at her side.

Hannah - "Stay, eat, I'll be back soon."

But we left, promising to return.

The next week Sue called to tell her we were coming over, but she was busy.

Sue - "So we'll make it another time?"

Hannah - "Sure. Another time."

Sue - "Maybe Wednesday?"

A bird of clear, distinct voice, one I had not heard recently, if at all, suddenly let out with a beautiful note followed by a few others. That was it, one song as Sue and I sat on the deck.

Tom - "He was there today. He spent a few hours with her, surprised that the family deferred to him. Here it is near the end and her mother said, 'You go.' She knew her daughter wanted to be with him."

Sue - "I know. He called earlier."

Tom – "He told me that he sat holding her hand. He recalled the labored breathing from his Mother's cancer, the limited lung capacity made worse by the morphine. He said 'I waited for the breath to stop, that's how it happens. But it didn't. She willed herself on, not that she was kidding herself. She knew what was happening, where she was going and why her sister and I were crying. She handed us the Kleenex.' "

Sue - "Amazing woman."

Sue and I went inside and called. She was gone. We wept.

Post script:

When a loved one gets sick, suffers and passes, we all ask, "Where is God? Why did this happen?" I don't think she dwelled on this. She accepted it and it became her mission to remind us, unselfishly, to stop fretting over the ridiculous, mundane, petty issues of this life. To be with our families and show them our love; to be forgiving and to enjoy each day, no matter what; to smell the flowers – in fact, plant a few; to love life as she did, even as it was leaving her. Thank you for being a part of our lives Hannah. We will always love and remember you.

September 5, 2002

Chapter Eight

Catskills in June

2007

Mack,

We stayed at the Riverside Lodge which lost a few cabins last year and had water 3 feet deep in its kitchen. No floods this year, at least not yet. The river is low and not so cool. I am with twenty nine guys from Long Island looking for some trout.

Jerry and I arrived a day early and fished the afternoon and evening hatch, or what there was of one, on the Cemetery Pool. Last year I had a monster on at the bottom of the pool but had to break it off as the river was too high and strong for me to follow him after he exhausted my backing. The same spot this year had about 18 inches of water and no fish.

Friday morning we went to the Sunoco Pool, right next to the lodge. Jerry got into 5 nice fish and had a smile on his face. I had as many refusals. We headed up to the Willow and our favorite stretch. The area below has been renamed "Mansion Pool." Doesn't seem right to name a pool on this famous stream for such a newcomer.

The floods didn't change this section much as it still has deep water on each bank but what did happen is the stream below the parking lot was gouged out. I heard reports later in the weekend of good fishing all day long down there, but it is not where we wanted to fish. Even my "trick fish" which I can always tease out of his under the bank lair had apparently moved out, maybe to the big water downstream.

We headed back to the lodge and greeted some of the guys who were heading out. They suggested we try Ben Grey's or the Barrel Pool, just downstream. It is a nice stretch and certainly has fish but we struck out. We met for dinner and I managed not to over eat this year.

Discussion was where to go this evening and everyone was thinking West Branch of the Delaware where the water was cooler and more plentiful. The no-kill in Deposit was the target of too many so Jerry and I decided to go further upstream to Stilesville, just below the dam.

The air temperature was 91 on the car thermometer as we pulled into the parking spot. No one was in the river although there was another parked car. We climbed down the bank and it was like sticking your head in the freezer door. The air temperature dropped 20 degrees. It was refreshing. As we entered the stream the water chilled our legs. Tail water releases from the bottom of the reservoir.

We waded across and waited for a rise. One quickly accommodated us but only one. There were some bugs on the water and I tried a few patterns but nothing was moving except the fog. Because of the cool water and hot humid air, there was a low hanging fog swirling just above the water. As I looked upstream at Jerry he was appearing and disappearing, like one of those old English movies with the fog of London providing the atmosphere. I looked downstream and waves of fog were seemingly washing up on the far bank. It was a sight to see, but no fish. We stayed until almost dark and decided to try by the Plycom Pool, below town.

The floods had roared through here last year and the treatment plant on the other side of the river is still discharging chlorinated effluent into the river. What I did not expect was the immense amount of rock piled up on the bank where trees once were. 50 yards from the road to the water there is nothing but rocks. The character of the pools and the island which is just below the bridge had all changed. Peter and others from our group were on the island and having some luck. I waded in on this side and made a few casts but soon had a leader tangle that could not be set right so I called it a night.

Back at the lodge everyone was hanging out on the porch by our room while swarms of large stoneflies were climbing on everything and everyone. As cars came into the parking lot it looked like a light snow had fallen and the passage of the vehicle was throwing up a snowy spray but they were all stoneflies. As we opened the door to our room 10 or 20 came in and had to be dealt with before we could comfortably turn in for the night.

The next morning I walked to the Sunoco Pool and got in the river next to Rick who had just landed the fish of a life time: a brown over 20 inches. He caught him on a large stimulator, obviously imitating one of the now dying stoneflies. I had a few refusals and headed for breakfast.

I had heard of fishing for small brookies on a brook upstream and one time went up that way but ended up on another instead. Over breakfast I was speaking to the reel maker, Rich Bradley, asking him how he came to move up here from the Island and make custom fly reels. He was a machinist on the Island and worked for a few shops, including one owned by a guy he had no love for. He told me that he should have been put in jail for how he operated, and assured me that if it was him, he would be in jail. So much for blind justice.

Turning the conversation to more pleasant topics, I asked him where he'd suggest we fish the day with the rivers getting low and warm, as well as crowded. He suggested this little brook and gave me directions. I told Jerry we were going to a secret spot and he tried to guess but didn't come up with it. I missed the turn so we turned around and tried again. We passed the intended brook and pulled up to another which is off a gravel road and very secluded, although there were some wilderness camp sites here and there.

It was beautiful but very small. A gurgling brook, or was it babbling? I pulled over by a bridge used for snowmobiles. Jerry planned to fish the run just above it which had a rise before we even set up our rods. I worked my way upstream a half mile or so picking up a small brookie every 50 feet or so. In the bigger holes there were bigger fish, up to 6-7 inches. The repaired 6 foot, 3 weight bamboo (now 5'11" actually) was the perfect tool.

As I moved along I saw some folks hiking but they quickly disappeared. Then I heard what sounded like music, city music. I continued up as it became clearer and louder. Rap or hip hop, not sure I know the difference. A deadfall was ahead of me which made the brook turn and swirl. A nice pocket of deep water was the result. I was high above it and looking down where two nice size fish were working whatever was coming downstream. I moved closer and they scrambled for cover. I sat and waited. Eventually one came back out to look around, but then skittered back.

I tried to drop a fly in from above but it didn't tempt them from their cover. It also ended up hooked on a root. I climbed down to recover it, spoiling the hole, and moved upstream.

The music was now blaring. Around a bend was a camp site with a young couple setting up their tent. Bicycles at the ready and the door of their SUV open with the radio blasting. Why bother coming all this way when you are just going to bring the noise with you? I thought of what I would say if given the chance and then decided it would be better to just move on. I turned and worked my way back to Jerry.

We came upon Sol's Jeep parked at a trail head and I was reminded of a prank we used to play on friends when we saw their cars at the beach. We would take their hubcaps, (and anything else we could), and look forward to hearing their story of how they were ripped off. It was great fun as we played them to embellish the story and express their indignation, only to start laughing uncontrollably as they figured out the prank. Sol didn't have hub caps and it seemed too cruel to let the air out of his tires, so we headed for town.

We had a good dinner and listened to the plans of the others: who was going where and what they'd be using. Jerry had the idea of going up to East Branch by the bridge near the slate works. We had fished there before with Mickey and Moe with interesting results. It is where Moe took a bath and where a huge fish startled Jerry on his first cast. I had landed a very large brookie down below the bridge on a Mickey Finn fished into the debris.

When we climbed in, a modest walk down from the bridge, the water seemed deeper than we remembered, even with the reduced flow. Jerry seemed a bit peaked and was just standing there. He suggested I move upstream and that he would fish here. Something was not right. As I worked my way along the bank I glanced back to see him just standing there and later sitting. Concerned, I crossed the river and walked back feigning a nymph technique. When I reached him I asked if he wanted to try somewhere else and he said yes. We climbed the bank slowly and got back to the car. He was not feeling well but he was also not telling me.

I suggested we just call it a day and head back. He said no and suggested the Barrel Pool. When we arrived the spots were already covered by anglers and we had to walk a bit to squeeze into a location where success was going to be unlikely. We uncharacteristically bickered about where to set up. I was short on patience, probably due to my concern for his being bull headed about continuing when he wasn't feeling well.

I waited and watched for rises. He flailed away in hope of an opportunity. We moved to the bank near the road as one of the anglers left for the night. It was getting dark. Suddenly, not 10 feet from me, a splash, then another, and another. Four or five fish working right on top of us. I could not see anything on the water but needed to change to a dry fly. Then I remembered taking my new goose necked flashlight out of my vest to lighten it for a hot days' fishing. I figured a large rusty spinner would work and held my line to the sky in order to tie one on.

Nothing. Still they were rising. Jerry had moved in next to me and just watched. I put on a grey fox and nothing. The water was only 12 inches deep and these were good size fish. It got my heart thumping even though I didn't hook up.

We walked out and he admitted that he had forgotten to take a medicine he needs and it was making him feel weak and out of breath. When we got back he turned in and I went out to the annual camp fire. The guys had their instruments and the singing and chatter went on into the wee hours.

Sunday morning we slept in. After breakfast we said goodbye to everyone and headed for the Willow. Rhododendron Pool was our first stop. It had been rearranged by the floods but is still one of the most picturesque pools on the river. Jerry went down and I went up. I came across an old timer who had a cane which doubled as a wading staff. He was involved with Theodore Gordon Fly Fishers and was telling me of the politics at the Center and projects that needed to be done to help the rivers. He chatted on and finally gave me my leave pointing to a nearby rise. I waded out and hooked the fish, turned to smile at him but he was gone.

I rejoined Jerry who was enjoying working the newly formed riffle and undercut bank. We decided to move on. We discussed stopping at the Neversink by Holiday Mountain and the Old Homestead Restaurant. It was on the way home. We fished upstream of Route 17 just below the bridge. There were some arrogant little trout feeding voraciously just past a large rock at the head of the deep pool on the far side. I threw everything I had at them with no luck. I finally caught a tiny one on a sulfur emerger.

I gave the spot up to Jerry and moved downstream. I came upon a beautiful doe in the stream that looked at me a long while before heading for the bush. I thought it odd. As I continued to fish my way down I heard a sound almost like a crow cawing, but not quite. It continued and I looked above to try to identify the bird.

There was no bird. The sound became more of a baying, almost a call of Maa, Maa, Maa. Then I discovered the source. A fawn was struggling on the steep bank trying to follow its mother but could not get up. It wandered back and forth looking for a break in the bank but there was none. It finally settled down behind some grass which perfectly camouflaged it. It quieted down and was waiting for something to happen.

I considered helping it up the bank but wondered if I would hurt it or scare the mother off permanently. I also wondered if it would resist my Good Samaritan effort and bite me. I decided to just let nature figure it out.

I found Jerry tying on a new leader and smiling as he tightened the knot. These knots are a bitch to tie under normal circumstances and shaking hands don't help. We agreed to 15 minutes more, then dinner at the Homestead and home.

The time came to leave but the "just one more cast" syndrome kicks in even on trips where the fish gods have not been all that generous.

Hope springs eternal for a fisherman. I guess that's what I love about it.

Tom

Chapter Nine

Missoula to Jackson

2007

Mack,

Islamorada was a nice respite and it was fun being with my son and granddaughter for a few days without all the troubles that life presents. I managed a day and a half of tarpon fishing which was exciting fishing, without catching. I'd estimate that we saw 75 to 100 fish and I was able to cast to 20 or so with about 2 turning to look at the fly. I was on the saltwater, in the sun, perfect weather, and I had a fly line in the air, so how bad could it be?

We enjoyed the other benefits of time in the pool and at the various events our host arranged from a sunset luau to a pool side lunch of Mai-Mai that we hooked on a charter earlier that day, prepared in every way imaginable.

This trip was about as far from that tropical paradise as you can get, with cut rate motels standing in for the luxury of Cheeca Lodge. It was Jerry and I on a ten day, three stop tour starting in Missoula and ending in Jackson Hole.

Jerry's brother Danny had arrived the day before and met us at the airport after trying his luck on the Bitterroot. Fresh off the plane and in 105 degree heat we went to Rock Creek and drove to the 12 mile marker, a section I recalled from my trip in the mid 90's.

Rock Creek is about 40 miles long and is a tributary of the Clark Fork. When I was last there it was wild with very few homes and none on or near the river. Now there are not only multiple homesteads but signs everywhere asking the locals to fight the development of the valley.

As we traveled the dirt road along the river there were many good spots but all were challenging to enter with steep banks, given my elderly companions. We picked one and while we set up our rods, Danny took a ride upstream to see if there was a more friendly access. He found one by the suspension bridge with some promising water as well as two swimmers. By the time we got there, the girls were leaving and another fisherman had arrived who was smiling as the not unattractive ladies passed. I generally don't like places so many others frequent as it means the fish have been beaten to death with all sorts of flies. Also quiet, solo fishing is unlikely.

The three of us entered the river. Jerry hooked a fish in short order and was working on another. I followed with one coming up out of a rock crevice to a Purple Haze. I watched the other fisherman trying to walk along the rocks on the opposite bank in his street shoes, an older fellow with poor proprioception, nearly falling multiple times as he pursued the ideal place from which to cast. He hung up in a tree and then in a log, but fished on. I admired that. His lady was trying to film him from the bridge. I worked my way up my side and must have looked as clumsy to him as the rocks were large and the water deep.

I scrambled up and down to get to a better casting or dapping position, finally getting to one I was sure held great promise. I began to present my fly when a cheerful hello came from above. A young couple came down the bank and plopped directly in front of me, dangling their feet in the water. I suspected a PETA confrontation and decided to just retreat. So much for easy access.

I went downstream past Danny, working the pockets and riffles, raising a few small fish. I looked up to see Jerry reaching for his radio. For his last birthday I gave him a set of walkie-talkies so we could stay in touch on the stream. I could hear him asking how I was doing and what I was using but it was apparent he could not hear my response so I resorted to our usual signing. We later discovered he had the volume turned off. About 8 PM we packed it in and headed for dinner. We were about 30 miles from town and decided to eat at the Rock Creek Mercantile which was very good with a great salad bar.

The next morning we headed to the fly shop to meet our guide after a breakfast at Finnegan's which is built over Rattlesnake Creek and has the best pancakes in Montana. We met Roy at 6 AM to try to beat the heat of the day as well as the tubers and rafters who will populate the river in droves on a Saturday in the 100 plus degrees that were predicted.

He was a fellow from somewhere else who was knowledgeable and accommodating, even as his humor turned a bit dark. We followed his jeep up the Blackfoot River to the Johnsrud Park Access and put in. There were three of us in one boat plus the guide. It was not as bad as it sounds as long as you agree that only two can fish at a time. We doubled up on the front seat with one guy almost always standing while the other watched and shouted:

"You missed him."

The guy in the stern just fished as usual.

We fished with hoppers and small nymphs in a dropper set up, sometimes with three flies on a line. We had our share of tangles both with each other and with ourselves, but fewer than I would have expected. Later in the day, the guys in front switched to heavier nymphs – double beaded stoneflies. I stayed with a hopper and Prince Nymph. They caught more and bigger fish but I had my share of startling rises, refusals and takes including the last fish of the day as we pulled into the takeout within sight of US-90. Jerry was the high hook with at least 4 of them good size cutthroats.

We had visions of fishing the evening since the float came to an end by 3 PM, given the heat. Roy gave us some tips on where to go upstream from Johnsrud. One spot was about 6 miles up the dirt road until you come to a bridge, then turn around and go about 100 yards back downstream. Here the access was to be easy and the fishing good.

Back at the Super 8 we took our shoes off for a brief nap. If Danny had not banged on the door we would have surely slept the night through. We ate at The Depot, which was very good, and decided to take a drive to the Bitterroot instead of fishing. We passed through Florence and Danny directed us to a turnout where he thought we could easily see the river. It turned out to be a hike and the river was not only very low but filled with locals enjoying a dip and some fishing with their kids. One couple was walking back with what looked like a huge yellow perch on a stick and a big smile on their faces. The mosquitoes were hungry, driving us back to the car. The river was more than half bare rock and we wondered if it would be fishable further up as it was on our itinerary. I slept like a log that night.

Sunday we were at Finnegan's at 5:30 and in Roy's rig by 6. He talked of his fishing and hunting, of his friend who was a military sniper and their ability to shoot elk from 1000 yards away. There was a loose shotgun shell rolling around in the back and a .38 tucked into the pocket behind the front passenger seat. He went on about how he moved out here to get away from the diversity of America but it seemed to be following him. I guess he was preparing for the worst, whatever that might be. As it turned out he proved to be a skilled and accommodating guide with the patience of Job.

We briefly discussed where to fish. The Clark Fork was going to be very hot and full of people and the middle of the Bitterroot, as we saw, was very low due to irrigation demands plus a large tree had fallen across it where the boats usually drift and it would be tough to haul around. Apparently it is a wild and scenic river and it is allowed to remain natural even if it inconveniences those who support the wild and scenic designation. Everyone was bitching about it even as they benefit from the protections. It reminded me of when my sister petitioned to get a stop sign put on her corner only to be one of the first to be ticketed for ignoring it:

> "But you don't understand officer, it's my stop sign."

We decided to travel up the Blackfoot about 40 miles taking a 9 mile dirt road at River Junction into the wilds. We saw a herd of deer including a big buck with his rack in velvet as we bumped along. When we arrived, there were folks camping and a few float boats preparing to launch. This is the Blackfoot of Norman Maclean. The day was a repeat of the day before with wilder water and paddlers in wood strip canoes and kayaks. Our guide assured us they were all gay as were the ladies who waved to us from the bank. We caught fish and enjoyed a good lunch prepared and served with style, in spite of his homophobic observations.

We asked about the next day, as we had booked a third float thinking we would cover three different rivers. He advised we cancel it due to the low water and heat and suggested we go over to the Lochsa River in Idaho. It sounded good to us so we settled up at the shop.

Another good meal at The Depot followed by one of the highlights of Missoula: Big Dipper Ice Cream. We had passed the Carvel-like store a few times and wondered at the crowds lined up. It was delicious and unique as well as inexpensive. Don't miss it.

Our trip up Route 12 through Lolo Pass of Lewis and Clark fame began at a more leisurely pace. We were in a sightseeing mood and wanted to enjoy an extra hour's sleep as well. It is less than an hour's drive through the pass and into Idaho. Roy had described the waypoints accurately and we traveled about 15 miles downstream checking out various sites before turning around and selecting one to fish.

All were very scenic. Some had campsites where an honor system for use fees prevailed but so did ATVs. Almost everywhere we stopped in Idaho the four wheeled noise makers were present. We selected a spot which required a fairly steep climb but had very promising water, boulders and deep crevices, riffles and pockets. I hit a fish on a hopper immediately and he was nice enough to release himself before I could assess his size. I moved downstream hitting pockets, pillows and boulder slicks coming up with 5 or 6 more modest Westslope Cutthroats. I rejoined the guys and we moved upstream. After lunch we climbed down for more with all of us hitting fish, mostly modest in size but all tough to hook and land. It was getting late and we headed back, exploring another camp site before we hit the pass. It was a motor head haven so we moved on.

My allergies had been acting up for a few days and I finally figured out it was because of the smoke from the forest fires which were burning in a number of areas in Idaho as well as Montana and Wyoming. The drought and the heat had the fire meters along the highways all set at "Very High Risk." Jerry started to use a cup of water to put out his smokes to avoid making history.

Traveling back on Rt. 12 there is a shallow lake on the right probably formed by beaver dams. Trees line the highway but you can see it through the breaks. There is no shoulder on the road and traffic was heavier than you would have thought. I took a look at 50 mph and thought I saw one of the two reasons which make pulling off this winding road for a photo worthwhile, a moose or a bear. This was the former. I spun around almost parking on the road and we ran back to take a look. It was a big bull moose in the middle of the lake grazing on the underwater grasses. He ignored us as we gawked. Danny suggested we get closer and we moved up the road. He must have sensed the movement and less than stealth-like approach as he picked up his big head with full rack and moved back into the woods. Wow.

Although tired from the day of fishing, this reinvigorated us. There was one more road before the pass and it indicated another river access. We drove up to find more ATVs but also some kind of a building. It looked like a fish hatchery. We explored further and the holding tanks were filled with 24 inch or better Chinook salmon. We looked around and came across a young fellow who explained that these fish have navigated 9 dams, traveling 600 miles from the Pacific Ocean. They were captured as they tried to run up a tiny stream here at the head waters of the Lochsa and will be milked. The resulting fingerlings will be placed in a holding pond in order to maximize survival rate of these obviously genetically strong fish. The young will be imprinted at the pond and released in the spring run off to return to the sea. A hundred years ago the trip downstream would only take a few days. Now it can take months. They estimate that at each of the 9 dams they will lose a substantial number, leaving only a few to complete the trip and the cycle.

We fished two of the streams that form the Lochsa, the Crooked River and Dead Colt Brook which were filled with fish, natural cutthroats that is. Mostly small although Danny got into some larger ones. He also came upon a strange looking turbine like device anchored in mid-stream. We later found out that this is a fish counter.

There was a sign posted that a female moose had been sighted in the area with two calves and to be cautious. We were not so lucky as to see more than one moose this trip.

The next day Danny went back to Denver and Jerry and I to Ennis and the Madison River. We had a float planned for the next day through www.Grecosonthefly.com, Brett Greco's outfit. We arrived to the only rain we saw this trip, a brief shower, barely enough to keep the road dust down. We did some laundry, had buffalo burgers for lunch and looked around town for some souvenirs.

That afternoon we took a drive to the Ruby, a small brook which runs on mostly private land, including Ted Turner's massive ranch. Even with a map, we had some trouble locating the access points. Up a wrong road, we were almost run over by one of the biggest tractors I have ever seen. It was hauling hay and seemed to have little tolerance for wandering fishermen. We back-tracked to the gas station in Alder for directions and were on the water in a few minutes.

It was amazingly small but had good flow and was cold. They do not make getting to the Ruby easy as we had to climb under and around obstructions even though it was a public access. We spread out with me walking a ways upstream and Jerry following. Neither of us caught fish but they were there. I spooked at least one which skittered across a gravel bar, his back exposed, as I walked up. It was high noon and over 100 degrees, not to make excuses.

We were tired and headed back to Ennis around 4, stopping in Virginia City to look around. My memories of Bonanza and the Cartwright family came back to me as this old western town was the metropolis of that TV serial of the early 60's, the first color TV show as I recall, not that we had a color TV.

We met Matt, a guide who works with Brett, for a 6:30 AM start. We were going to put in at Lyons Bridge. It was cool enough to put on a sweat shirt for the first time since we had arrived although the weatherman assured us it would be over 100 by mid-day. The Madison is a brown and rainbow fishery, fish we are familiar with from the Delaware. Unlike the finicky cutthroats with their madding slow and soft takes, the browns and rainbows tend to be more aggressive, especially in fast moving water which is what we'd be in.

The Madison is a big river with counts of over 1500 fish per mile, and they tend to be big. We were in for a good day. Matt suggested dry flies all the way with a hopper followed by a smaller fly. Mine was a size 16 mahogany spinner and Jerry's a caddis. We both hooked up quickly. We had to adjust to Matt's system of straight casts with no mending which took a while after Roy's coaching to do the opposite. In both cases we had to keep the lines ahead of the boat and drag-less, watching intensely for a rise and ready to strike. I can't count the number fish that came up and took a look only to turn in refusal.

On the Blackfoot there were more rises followed by missed strikes than here. On the Madison once they decided to take, it was an event. Bam. Jerry caught a bunch of large browns, a few rainbows and lost even more. At one point he fished the pillow in front of a large rock and hooked a monster who tried to turn the boat around. Even with 4x tippet he couldn't drag him to the net. Another time he had one on that literally bent the hook to get off, all this on his 50 year old Hardy reel with hardly any backing. We pulled out at McAtee Bridge.

The river was busy but not crowded. Everyone seemed to know how to keep their distance. There were several couples fishing as well as a few boats with just women. Also a father and son were having their trip recorded by professional photographers, or videographers, in a pontoon boat which kept leap-frogging us to set up for the next shot.

There were plenty of antelope and deer as well as the unwelcome sight of new homes built on the flood plain where once there was only grass and wind. What benefit could there be to ruining the vista of this magnificent valley? Is it so important to sleep in sight of the river for one week a year? I am certain that my sons and grandchildren will never see the view of the Madison Valley which has amazed people for centuries. They will see man at his selfish worst filling it with seldom used houses, not homes, and then the rest of what comes with them.

That night we had a good meal at The Reel Decoy, a new place with great ribs and better pie. After, we explored the Valley Garden fishing access. The map shows the river in braids at this point and it was not apparent to us how we could navigate them without a boat. We decided to go to the movies instead. Like in the days of my youth, there was a small, single feature, popcorn-smelling theater in town with an 8 PM show of a new Pixar cartoon of a rat who would be a chef. It was fun. It brought back memories of going to a show when camping on the Beaverkill with my Dad, just to get out of the rain for a few hours: Kirk Douglas in *The Vikings* released in 1958. I'll have to rent it one of these days to complete this nostalgic voyage.

It is now July 19th and we are heading for Jackson. We plan to go to the headwaters of the Madison first and fish "the Barns" where Jerry caught fish many years ago. I also wanted to see Old Faithful and the Inn, a point of interest according to the GPS.

The trip took us through the rest of the Madison Valley and I showed Jerry $3 Bridge and told him of our time at Slide Inn, on Cabin Creek and at Mile Marker 13 along with the other water we fished while he was in Italy.

We stopped at the Blue Ribbon Fly Shop to seek their advice. The guys told us to forget the Park. The rivers were closed after 12 noon and the fishing wasn't good anyway, too hot. They advised we push on to Jackson to try our luck.

We stopped at MacDonald's in West Yellowstone to use the facilities and get a cup of coffee. The girl that served me was from Russia. The world keeps getting smaller.

Last year when traveling with Peter to the Yellowstone River I wanted to swing past Old Faithful. He argued that the road to the north was both shorter and more

picturesque, so we skipped it. I was looking forward to
seeing it this year. When we arrived, the famous geyser
was not due to blow for an hour. We looked around,
bought some more trinkets and left for Jackson. There is
always next year.

Yellowstone ends and Grand Teton National Park begins
followed by the Bridger-Teton Wilderness and other
preserves. The first view of the Tetons at the edge of
Jackson Lake is breathtaking, far beyond what a photo can
show. There was smoke from the fires hazing the view but
it was still spectacular.

Just a side comment on RVs: I always thought that
campers, of which RVers are a subset, were basically nice,
home spun, good old American pie kind of folks. Just
people trying to enjoy nature with their families. I excuse
their penchant for running generators all night to cool their
abodes while I curl up in my tent, trying to listen to the
crickets.

To put this next observation in perspective, you should
know that road rage is one of the many issues that I try to
work on continuously. I'll often pull over to let a too close
tailgater pass me by without flipping him the bird or just
stop and wait a while if the guy ahead of me is sliding
between 19 and 22 mph in a 30 mph zone with no passing.

I did not expect RVers to be like those drivers but here we
are on Rt. 89, two lanes with no passing for miles and then
passing zones with cars coming in the other direction most
of the time. An RV we were kind enough to let on to the

highway in front of us back in the Park slows to below 50 (speed limit is 55 to 75 depending) in the areas we cannot pass and as soon as a passing zone comes up he zips it up to 65.

At first I thought I was imagining it, looking for something to occupy my mind on the last leg of a five hour trip, but it happened again and again. Why? I told Jerry of my observation and let him know that rather than continuing this game with him, which I would ultimately have to win at all cost, I was going to slow down and enjoy the view. We ended up behind him again in Jackson, but it didn't matter anymore. I fantasized about pulling alongside of his rig and explaining what an ass hole he was but decided to let it go.

Jackson (or Jackson Hole as the Chamber of Commerce calls it) was jammed with traffic and no vacancy signs at every hotel. It is a good size tourist town and was filled to capacity. Rafting trips, hot air balloons, trail rides, mountain biking, kayaking and chair-lift rides dominated the activities. We stayed with Tom Bodette and had a poolside room. I was thinking that this will not be much of a wilderness experience.

After unloading the car we found the fly shop we had selected to do our float and met the owner and our guide, Ron. Something was uncomfortable about the place and the people. We asked Ron for directions to the Hoback River while he picked out some flies:

"Go to the junction, bear left, look for the moose (the steel one) and as you come into the canyon area pick a spot."

So we did. It was a nice stream with glacier blue water and enough pockets and boulders to make it interesting. We each caught some small cutts and I was beginning to explore some deeper water when I realized it was our agreed to meeting time.

Long Islanders Peter and Tommy along with ex-Islander and current Las Vegas guy, Bill, had arrived and we headed to Bubba's for dinner. It was good to see some friends and we shared our adventures to date with them over pulled pork and ribs followed by the special: buttermilk pie. Smooth cheese cake like filling made from the named milk in a homemade crust, delicious.

The guys had just driven in from Salt Lake and were exhausted. We bid each other a good sleep and turned in. I made the mistake of turning on the TV and *Good Fellows*, (one of my favorites), was on AMC. We forced ourselves to watch it in spite of the annoying commercials which are more frequent and seem longer and louder as the movie winds down.

Breakfast at Bubba's was as good as the dinner and we were at the fly shop at 9 AM. With the temperature only in the 90's I guess there was no need to start earlier. We had three boats as the shop would not accommodate a boat of three. Jerry and I choose to fish the somewhat quieter water, putting in at Astoria Hot Springs. The other guys went down to the white water where all the rafters go.

Matt, our guide on the Madison, was constantly jumping out to slow down the float or rowing from one side to the other to put us in the best position for fish. This guy was okay but not working too hard. He went to Penn State and played a season or two for Joe P. (I told him I had his brother George as a high school coach but he didn't seem impressed.) He said he was a real star in high school as a tail back but lost interest in college:

"Been guiding and hunting ever since."

He moved out here with his bride (which he said was a good thing as the male to female ratio is 8 to 1).

Fishing on these rivers from a float boat can be exhausting. When you are wading, especially in the east, you generally look for a rise to fish to, or at least work a likely looking spot with your fly. You watch it carefully during its fairly short drift and then reconsider where to put it next.

Out here, in a boat, your drifts can be a hundred feet long and more since the boat is moving with the river. Because of the terrain and the high population of fish, you are almost always in a zone where something can happen, you dare not take your eye off the fly. You can fall into a Zen-like trance by staring at the fly, recasting, mending, staring, waiting, constantly alert to the fact that it can happen. The fish can rise and take the fly at any moment and you need to be ready.

Do this for a few hours over a few days and you'll see what I mean by exhausting. Of course when it happens, when he reacts to the fly, when he comes up to take a look or even mouths it, you forget the tedium of the hunt and fill with renewed energy, sometimes too much as you strike too fast or too hard.

I love seeing the fish, hooked or not. I count coop on them. Just having tricked them out of their lair is enough for me although feeling the tug, tug, tug and landing a beautiful native is always nice. I saw fish all day, every day this way, by watching the fly. I hooked only a small percentage of those who rose and landed even fewer. What a great sport.

The float was over by 2:30 in the afternoon which seemed a little early. We got to see the Snake River and the cutthroats but Jerry summed it up as a bust.

When we were at the fly shop settling up, the owner whispered to me:

"Was Ron okay?"

I didn't like or trust the guy so gave him a non-committal shrug.

When we met up with the other guys for dinner they said they had a great day which bummed us even further. Upon eliciting the details, theirs was much like ours with few hook ups and the added adventure of having rafters bumping into them. I felt better about our day.

We had a good meal at the Gun Barrel which the guide had recommended – I had elk steak and some very good cherry cobbler. We asked our guide for information on where to fish the next day. He suggested two spots, one on the Snake, upstream near the dam, and the other on the Gros Ventre (pronounced Gro-Vont). The other guides were less helpful with both restaurants and fishing spots, so I was beginning to feel better about our tailback.

Our plan was to have breakfast at "89" and fish the Snake during the day and then have lunch on our way to the Gros Ventre.

We had rented a brand new Nissan minivan in Missoula with less than 6000 miles on it. I noticed the brake light was on as we headed out Saturday morning. I set and released it once but the light stayed on. I decided to ignore it. Then the battery light came on. Again, I ignored it, after all, it's a new car.

The walk into the Snake from the Lower Schwabacher Landing turnoff of Rt. 89 was flat but long and the day was hot. Jerry had some trouble with it and we almost aborted. The other guys went ahead and radioed us back that we were close. Once there, Jerry seemed better.

There was a ton of animal droppings in this place called the Antelope Flats. I am sure elk, deer, moose and bear as well as snakes share it with the antelope. It was covered with scrub brush, a few pine trees and old deciduous trees struck down by a long ago flood or storm, and bleached white and gray, the Tetons in all their glory right in front of us.

We spread out and tied on various offerings. Mine was a hopper and caddis combo from the day before. I fished the seam without entering the water after picking up a few small ones close to the bank. I kept trying to get a drag-less float about 20 yards out. I worked at it with casts and mends and finally achieved what I was looking for when the fish hit. No easy taker, this one. I was so excited to have a good size fish on, the first one since we were up on the Madison. He fought, came and ran, came and ran again. I sensed him tiring and tried to force him in so he would not be exhausted when released. He came to the surface and as I attempted to skitter him in, he shook, spit and was gone, a good fish.

There were others that rose to the flies and a few that took, but none that were like him. Upstream, one was chasing something to the surface and smashing it then rolling back to the bottom, another big fish. I watched, tied on a caddis and tried to remember where he last came up but it was never the same place twice. These fish were tough. They give you one shot at hooking them and never seem to rise a second time without a long, long rest. At the agreed hour, we strolled back to the cars for some lunch.

On the way back, I took my time looking at the interesting rocks. Most had unique colors and many had a white stripe on them, as if a layer of white ash had settled on the valley of their formation. We also saw fossils on some of the larger stones. I explored the creek that went by the parking area which had a marshy side channel and a pond of sorts where a moose could enjoy a meal. I'd like to come back in the early morning or evening to see what there was that made so much poop.

It was after 3. We had sandwiches from the grocery store but no shady place to sit, so we decided to drive up the Gros Ventre and eat there. I led the two car caravan to the junction and we drove 12 miles, past Kelly and toward Slide Lake, on a narrow dead-end, now dirt, road with nothing but dude ranches ahead. Then the car started to act up. The transmission seemed to be slipping out of gear. I stopped and fiddled with the gas pedal. I thought for a moment that my big wading boot was hitting the brake and the gas at the same time. It has happened before. I put it in gear and we continued on.

The road was climbing and narrowing. We were at the apex of a hill above the lake where only one car could go at a time. It happened again. We all took a look and started to speculate about what was happening. A car wanted to pass and another was coming up the other way. I got the van to roll forward and pulled over as close to the cliff as was reasonable. Peter, whose cell phone always seems to work, tried to call the car rental agency but was put on hold until the signal dropped. A nice family in a pick-up stopped but had no jumpers or phone and didn't know where they were. Then a cowboy in a big red pickup jumped us and we let it charge a short while, too short.

He passed on the information that the river was too hot to fish, which was a small consolation. Jerry and I jumped in and went down the road to turn around. Peter advised that we race for the airport where we could exchange the car. We had determined that the alternator must have gone which drained the battery which was needed to run the electronic transmission. Even with the engine running, if the alternator wasn't generating electricity or recharging the battery, it was only a matter of time before the transmission would cut out.

I drove like a bandit on this dirt road but only made it about a mile before it died again. As luck would have it, we were at a turn out with a fishing access. We radioed the other guys who were right behind us. The plan was for Tommy and Peter to fish here while Bill drove Jerry and I to the airport car rental. At the town of Kelly I picked up a signal and called service. I was on hold until we literally pulled up to the curb at the airport. The guy was of little help or encouragement. We went inside to the counter where a lady took care of us, gave us another car and told us they would not charge us for the near empty gas tank on the Nissan. Miracles do happen.

At breakfast the next day we retold our story as the guys smiled and eventually filled us in on a great evening of fishing on the Gros Ventre. Lots of good size fish on small flies. It came back to me that this was the location the guide had told us to fish. We had pushed past it looking for a waypoint which we must have missed. The car breaking down here brought us to the right spot. Sometimes things work out.

After breakfast, we bid everyone adieu and headed for the airport and home. Exhausted and well rested at the same time, we looked forward to a night in our own beds. As we sat on the runway I asked:

"Where do you want to go next?"

He responded:

"West Branch of the Delaware in September."

"Good."

Tom

Letters to Mack

Chapter Ten

4 AM with the Boys

2007

Mack,

It is August and we are over at my son Tom's as they prepare for their vacation on the beach in North Carolina next week. I am glad his two buddies and their families can go as well. It should be a great time, especially with 6 kids and three such good friends.

I am fretting that by the time they return summer will be all but over, and although we have had fun with the boys, I still want more. This being the case, I ask them if they want to go fishing with me before they leave. They say:

"Sure, when?"

"How about 4 in the morning Tuesday?"

103

"Great" they say and ask their Dad if it's okay.

I really didn't want Tom to have to get up at 4, even though I know he would, so I suggest they sleep over:

> "That way we can be on the boat fishing before the first light."

They ask again and it's okay. I have been out at 4 in August and it can be stunning, both in beauty as well as in the number of fish moving on the surface. I hoped for a good day as we made final plans.

I picked them up Monday afternoon with their wheelie suit cases in tow and we headed for the Neck. After a good dinner, shared with their cousin Sarah who didn't stay the night, we headed for bed. Sue asked if I was really going to go out at 4. I confessed that I'd get up but would wake them closer to 4:15.

It didn't take much to rouse them. A quick shake and they were both on their feet and pulling on their clothes. I handed out the flashlights and we headed for the dink.

We were under way by 4:45. The bay was like a sheet of glass, but no bunker jumping. We cruised around and trolled a bit hoping to pick up some blues, but nothing. I headed out to the porgy spot off the lighthouse and after not too long they both had fish in the boat. Hunter's a good sized porgy of well over 2 pounds, I'd say.

As we were dropping our lines for another round, the birds showed up between us and the point. Suddenly there were bunker on the surface followed quickly by some smashing blues. I snagged a bunker and let Hunter hold the pole as I set Shane up to flip a plug out with the spinning rod.

Exciting, but no hook ups. And then, as happens, they were gone. We waited and they came up again. And then again, but no connects. It got quiet, but the boys no longer wanted to porgy fish.

We headed toward the stacks as the sun began to burn off the morning fog and the first breeze riffled the surface. I hoped to entice some of those small bass that hang out in the warm water from the power plant to come up for the plug. The boys were getting hungry and a granola bar was not going to do it.

> "How about the Shipwreck Diner?" was Hunter's suggestion.

I agreed and we headed to town.

As we came into the harbor the bunker school that usually hangs out across from the Northport Yacht Club was agitated. They were swimming in circles on the surface, and each fish had to go a pound or so. The girls from the sailing school were mustering in the channel, waiting for their class to start, and were as amazed at the scene as we were.

I snagged a few for the bucket and then let one swim on the treble hook. Meanwhile Shane was intent on casting his plug into the school. He moved to the bow where he would be less likely to hook Hunter (or me) as he flipped his plug - very well, I might add. Good distance, good retrieve. I was proud. My boys were really becoming fishermen. Then all hell broke loose.

The blues started massacring the school all around us. The bunker on the hook, which Hunter was holding, was quickly bitten in half and they were coming up like fish in a hatchery to the bloody chunk.

Shane kept casting and to his surprise a blue grabbed his Atomic Bomber and began to run. He was on the bow and screaming with joy. I walked him into the cockpit and had him lean into the gunwale for stability. He cranked the reel and the fish took more line.

Back and forth, up and down, jumping and diving. Then it decided to go under the boat and Shane, hanging on to the pole for dear life, watched as the fish twisted the rod around and bent it under the boat. I coached him, screamed really:

> "Keep it off the rail. Don't let the rod touch the boat."

If it did, it would have broken in two. The fish came back up and I got the net on him.

Hunter ran for the ruler and we measured him at 30 inches, a big fish. Bigger than the tackle Shane was using would normally handle but he landed him just the same. A McCoy record. (Not as big as Sue's, which is the absolute biggest blue fish any McCoy ever caught or ever will catch, but a record for Shane.) His first hooked and landed by him alone on light tackle. What a thrill.

We chunked and plugged some more but the blitz was over. The boys remembered their stomachs and we went to town for egg sandwiches, talking all the while of our battle and victory and how exciting it was and how we needed to eat fast to go do some more.

They didn't want to go in that day, even after 7 hours on the water and no more fish since breakfast. I think they are hooked.

Tom

Letters to Mack

Chapter Eleven

Four Peaks

2007

Mack,

Every year I have this urge to get upstate and hike a few mountains. It's not a rational thing but emotional, like a calling - maybe spiritual. Whatever it is, I try to give in to it.

I didn't make firm plans but rather just waited until the day before to mention it to Sue and she was supportive, as always. I called Keene Valley Lodge to see if they had a room:

> "Yes, number 1, a double with a private entrance and bath."

Tom and I stayed in this room when we went up a few years ago. They gave it to me for the single rate. Good deal. No need to call the others on my list.

I pulled out my gear and packed what I needed for both hiking and fishing, but I could not find my boots. I looked high and low and finally recalled leaving them at Tom's when I was gardening there. He was in North Carolina with the family and my niece was house sitting. Since she is a late sleeper I didn't want to go over and scare her by rummaging through the garage at 7 AM, so I headed up bootless figuring I'd stop at the Mountaineer in Keene Valley and get a new pair.

I left in no particular hurry and found myself over the Tappan Zee by 11. I had a burger on the thruway and made it to Keene by 2:30. Checked in, which really means I walked into my room and dumped my stuff. The key was on the dresser. I looked at the list of other guests in the living room, but none were familiar.

The store is only a few doors down. The boot selection had changed since I bought my last pair there 10 years earlier. Everything looked like a sneaker. I tried on the Solomon's in a few styles as the salesman said they accommodated big wide feet like mine. I thought they were comfortable but the guy kept saying:

> "Do your toes touch the front when you walk down the ramp? You won't be happy if they do."

How do I know if they touch? I hate buying shoes. I am not connected to my feet like other people are. I endure them rather than nurture them. I try to break shoes in, to work with them, rather than pursuing the ideal of getting shoes that actually fit. The only pair of shoes I bought in my life that fit, that actually felt good, were the ones I got in Düsseldorf when we were walking the city and all I had were my business shoes. They were the best. I nicknamed them "Happy Feet" long before the movie. I have never found as comfortable a shoe since and I don't expect to.

So after walking around the store, up the stairs, up and down the ramp and taking them off, putting them back on and doing it again, I am thinking they are okay, but he keeps saying:

"…you won't be happy."

So I ask to try the leather ones. They are heavy he says. I feel them and of course they are heavier than the sneakers, but so what? I'm tough enough for heavy, it's the fit I am looking for. I put them on and my feet make an audible sigh of relief. There is room, but they are stiff - and a bit heavy.

For the sake of making a decision, even if it's a bad one, I go with the leather and ask if I can wear them out. He says I can but I can't bring them back if they are used, which made no sense to me. Of course they are going to get used, what the hell do you think I am buying them for?

At the register the guy says, as a final warning:

"They are stiff, make sure to give them time to break in."

Right.

It's now almost 4 so I need a short hike to break in the boots and my body. I usually do Baxter Mountain but have done it 4-5 times so decide to do Owls Head. I have passed it many times and always wondered about it. The fellow in the store said it's a good short climb with some nice views.

It fit the bill so I lightened my pack for a short climb. The trail entrance is marked with two logs and big brown and yellow sign that says "trail" with an arrow, but I ask a lady sitting in her car where it is. She was kind enough to be gentle:

"See the sign with the arrow over there…"

I headed up, what amounted to a stair case, to the top.

That night I stopped in at Fran Better's Adirondack Sport Shop. He finally moved his trade mark sign of the girl across the street to the new building. He was eating his dinner at his tying desk and we exchanged pleasantries. I asked for a dozen Usuals in 12 and 14 and noticed some large Ausable Wulffs with tall wings on his desk. I had to have a few of them as well. As always, when asked how the fishing is he replies:

"The fishing is fine, if you know what you're doing."

I shouldn't have asked.

I settled for a milk shake for dinner and got on the stream at my favorite spot, just above the gorge, and there was not even one car. I had the place to myself and fished down through the boulders picking up a few fish with the new Wulffs. There were huge flies in the air, many of them coupled together, so I tried a large spinner and had a hit. I think they were mating Isonychias.

The next morning, at the B&B, I had breakfast with a lady and her daughter from Virginia. A past school principal and now recruiter, we talked about the difficulty of getting teachers into low paying areas from places like Long Island. They were up for a memorial service for a relative with a house at the Ausable Club who had a large flower garden which they were weeding on her behalf, and bitching about it. I wanted to ask if I could come pull some weeds, never having experienced "The Club."

I selected Hopkins as my climb of the day. A good size hill but not too challenging, and it was close by. A little over 3 miles up, some of it along the East Branch and Mossy Cascade Brook. I went in just east of the bridge. There is an alternate route, walking up a dirt road just to the west, but I'd recommend this one which puts you in the woodsy state of mind quicker. After a short while, I came to the road with the red house on the left. There were people about and a barking dog. I made my turn to the right leaving the river and following the brook, a small one with many miniature falls. The guide book advised taking a side trip to see what they call "The Falls" but with the limited August flow I decided to just press on.

The woods were serene with little wind. The babble of the brook combined with the cadence of my steps lulled me into a trance. I walked myself right off the trail and into someone's yard. I back tracked and found a wooden bridge across the brook, but this was not in the ADK guide book. There were some yellow paint marks but no official trail badges. I crossed and passed an outhouse and what I think was a well, when I decided to turn around.

As I headed downstream, (or down-brook), a noisy bunch was hopping across the water on well-placed rocks and zipping up the trail. I grumbled to myself, preferring the quiet and not caring for the competition triggered in my addled brain by someone ahead or behind me. I sat for a while and watched the water gurgle over the rocks, moving to get different perspectives of the same flow.

Back on the trail, the pitch increased and at one point those yellow paint marks intersected with the trail, perhaps being some local's (or more likely a seasonal resident's) short cut. I passed a portly lady who was walking down. She smiled and said she only walked to the first outlook since she was hiking alone and didn't want to go all the way to the top. I admired her effort and wished her good day.

The first view came at a rock outcropping. I sat to cool off and have a drink. Since crossing the brook I had been pacing myself carefully. I was taking my pulse periodically trying to keep it under 130. This called for a rest every 100 yards or so, given this vertical section, making this a slow climb to be sure.

The noisy troop passed me on the way down, still zipping along; a bunch of young people in sneakers caring more for their conversation than their footing. Alone again.

What should be 4.5 hour round trip took me 3 hours one way but I didn't feel badly about it. There were two women and a few kids at what looked like the peak, so I sat among the blueberries and gazed at the view, planning to move over when they left, which they did shortly. My new boots had served me well in supporting my ankles but my toes were feeling a little off. I took a look and there were no blisters, just an uncomfortable sensation. I chalked it up to breaking them in.

The guide book talks of the blueberries as if you could bake a pie with them, or survive on them if you were stranded. At this altitude and in this climate, with no sustainable water to nurture them, they are dwarf both in the size of bush and berries, so if you go, don't bother to bring your picking basket.

The trip down took an hour and a half, matching the round trip expectations set. My feet were uncomfortable and I was looking forward to slipping into my boat shoes. As I neared the East Branch I stopped to watch the water for fish. I thought I saw a rise and marked the spot for later.

After some chicken and biscuits at the Noonmark Diner, I decided to take it easy and fish the East Branch rather than driving 30 miles to the West. It was warm so I left my vest in the car carrying a few implements and one box of flies: Adams, Usual and Ausable Wulffs along with a few nymphs and streamers. When I got in the river I noticed that the red house, the one with the barking dog, was positioned directly in front of me about a half mile away on a high overlook where the river takes a sharp left turn. What a great location. Far enough into the woods to be peaceful yet near the highway for access and on the stream. I envision them sitting in the different seasons watching as the river transforms from torrent to trickle, seeing the trout rise and the identifying the mayflies in the spider webs on their porch lamps. I could do that.

I started downstream of the bridge, working all the runs and pools patiently. Some were so slow moving that I could have placed my rod on a rock and taken a nap while my fly worked its way through. I plucked at the pockets and ran the runs as I moved up, in no particular hurry. Nothing was showing. 7:30 came and went and 8:30 was approaching, as was the dark. I turned and reworked the likely spots. There was a large boulder in mid-stream (well, mid-stream when there is water in it, mid-stream bed at this time of year). It had a pool behind it with some depth. A trout had to be in there. I sat and watched for a while and then flipped in the Wulff. It sat in the eddy swirling, given the long leader I had on, and then sank. I

116

repeated a few times selecting a different point to begin each time. On the 4th or 5th attempt, just before I was ready to move on, a brown came up and smacked it. A nice 10 inch specimen, I thanked him for making my evening and walked out with the smile.

As often as I have walked these woods, I have never climbed one of the "high" peaks. There are 46 peaks (or 47 depending on how you measure) over 4000 feet in the Adirondacks. There are people who conquer them all and wear a patch to let others know. There are some who run up and down them all.

I understand the obsession with achievement of personal goals but I don't use mountains to fulfill mine, not that it's a bad thing. Life has enough challenges for me at sea level. I need the mountains to refresh and cleanse, so I avoid thinking about being a 46'er. Cascade appealed to me because I have been to the lakes that lie at its foot. Cousin Tom and I caught fish there on purple martins and Mepps spinners. He and his Dad would take the canoe and use live killies to catch the big ones on the bottom.

I pass the crowded trailhead parking areas, which flank both sides of the highway, every time I go to the West Branch or Lake Placid. I read about it and the guide book said it was the easiest of the 46 to climb. Easy, I found, must be a relative term.

I put on my boots and had an early breakfast without conversation. I was parked at the trail head by 8:45 and there were already 7 cars. Perhaps some were campers. I switched from a ball cap to a bandana reasoning that the head is known to let heat escape from your body, which is why you cover it in the winter. I sprayed my thinning dome with sun screen and clipped my cap to the pack. I stopped at the registration kiosk to sign in but the trail book had long ago been filled. I should have left a note in my room or told the cook where I was climbing today.

The easy walking soon came to an end as the trail began to resemble a steep stream bed without water. I took my time, stopping often, checking pulse, cooling off and taking a sip. Before too long a fellow and elderly woman passed me coming down, then another and a few more. That accounted for 4 or 5 of the cars. I considered the hope of having the peak to myself. The climb continued to be steep and challenging for me. I came to the crossroad sign indicating the path to Porter, only .7 miles, Cascade was .2 more. The beginning of the granite peak was just ahead and I carefully clawed my way up only to find that I was at the beginning of what was considerably more granite elevation to climb.

As I sat to catch my breath and contemplate how to proceed; I took a look at the guide book which advised keeping to the slashes painted on the rock. There were a few cairns of rocks and pebbles several feet high from those who had been here before me and I told myself that if others could do it, so could I. The yellow slashes wove a path over the granite which, at first look, didn't seem to have any advantage over any other route. They all looked difficult. I took off my pack, put my camera in my pocket and then sat, somewhat afraid to continue.

A couple came up behind me, she with a cast on her arm. He left her at the foot of the rock and scampered up along the indicated route. I watched. When he came down, I got up the courage to try.

To complicate things, there was a big wind, had to be 20 - 30 mph or better, gusts even higher. (I later found out that it was so bad that it caused a tornado in near-by Vermont.) I kept a low profile and stayed on all fours making my way up. Progress disclosed more elevation and steeper rock. I stood, letting the wind dry my body from the climb and took in the view, thinking:

"Maybe this is far enough."

Then the 4000 foot thing came into my mind:

"Sure, come all the way to here and still don't get to claim at least one of the 46'ers."

It's a disease, this drive. I look again at the peak and there is another couple coming toward me.

"How high is this thing?" I wonder, as they were out of my sight just a minute ago.

She was dressed like she was cross country skiing (in August) with poles and parker. When we met they asked if I would take their picture. They were from Quebec and warned me to watch the gusts. They took my picture and I

119

pressed on. Shortly I came to the US Survey marker at the summit. I did it.

After lingering at the top for a while I made my way down to the edge of the granite. By that time there were more people clamoring up the trail and bivouacking prior to the final ascent. Ten, fifteen, maybe twenty people. Kids from 8 to teenagers, parents, singles, pairs, it was a day at the beach for these people. One girl was even climbing barefoot. My Mount Everest was their mole hill. Humility was required.

I sat and freed my feet which had been hurting since the beginning of the climb. My second toe had developed a blister, so I aired them out for a while and clipped the nail that I thought may have caused it, pretending it was not the boots. Put on a Band-Aid and extra pair of socks, ate lunch and started down.

I passed more and more people, some with even younger children. An older gentleman with a large format camera and walking stick aided by a not that much younger comrade was unruffled by his climb. More people passed. I saw one and only one who had broken a sweat and was toweling himself off at the crossroads. Finally, someone to whom these mountains bring the perspiration of a good work out to, as they do me.

I have never climbed more than three peaks in any of my trips to these mountains. In fact, two is what I usually can do. I just did my first 4000 footer and now I have the opportunity to do my second in only .7 miles. Porter.

How can I pass this up, blister or not? I take a look at the trail description in the book and it indicates a steep dip and then a climb with moderate views from the peak. I figured that I would not do this trail again since there are so many more to take. Chances are if I don't do it now, I never will. I turn left.

As I am heading down the described dip I am thinking about having to climb back up. I reach the bottom and the upside is not so bad. I come to the big rock and go up to get the view. With tentative footing and nothing to grasp, it offers its own little challenge but I am more inclined toward courage after seeing all those kids and senior citizens.

The peak is a small out cropping and it is crowded. I sit for a short while, rotating to look at each point of the compass. It was worth it. I snap a photo of a fellow standing on top of the adjacent Cascade and start my descent.

I went back to Wilmington to pick up a few more of those Ausable Wulffs and had a burger at the ice cream stand before heading for the river. I went to the same spot, not feeling the need to see a new stretch as I did last year.

Again, the pull off was empty and I had the river to myself. I was working the upper pool, knowing that the fish would come later, when a fellow joined me. I invited him to move into the pool and to feel free to follow me downstream if he'd like. He was new to the area, from

Connecticut, and seemed a likeable sort. I told him of my experience two nights ago and offered him a Usual.

We both went fishless until after 7:30 when I had some rises to my fly, but no hook ups. I worked the pool and missed a few more, changing from the Wulff, which was showing more wear than a new fly should, to an Adams and then a Usual. I reversed my direction and moved upstream of my new friend who got into the pool and hit four fish. I had two and missed one huge one. I took my leave as he fished on in the dark, inspired by the fruits of the Ausable.

I decided to have a leisurely breakfast and head for home rather than squeezing in another climb. I had already broken my record with four peaks this trip and my feet were sore.

On the way down the Northway I thought of things family and people past. It occurred to me that I had never gone back to see Lake St. Catherine, where I spent two or three summer vacations as a child.

I stopped above Lake George, gassed up and bought a map of Vermont. That's right, a map. Paper printed on both sides and folded into 16 parts or so. I love maps, in spite of the GPS on my dashboard.

The lake is in the town of Wells, just across the New York border, almost due east from the southern tip of Lake George. I took the detour.

There was a small lower lake on which our cabin sat and a general store in town. I recalled all the yellow perch we caught and the fish fry we would have on Friday it being pre Vatican II. The dock for swimming and the smell of a 15 horse power Johnson my Dad would bring to put on the row boat. I remembered talk of the men going up to the big lake for bottom dwelling lake trout and us swimming across the lake behind the second row boat we would rent, this one motor-less.

I found where the former Lyn-Are resort stood (named for daughters Lynn and Clare). It is now all private homes. Most of the cabins have been remodeled or replaced. I parked on the road which used to border the swamp. At some point the stream that exited from it was dammed and a lake resulted, albeit a shallow one - more water front property for the realtors. I walked slowly looking for clues.

I came to a lane which ran parallel to the lake with houses facing the lake on both sides, offering a double tier of lake view homes. As I walked, a woman came out to water her garden. I asked if she knew of the cabins that once were. She said no, but her neighbor's father owned them.

With her permission, I walked to the lake in front of her home and stood reminiscing, trying to pick up the vibrations of so many years before. I headed back in-between the houses when her neighbor came out. I got up the courage to introduce myself. She was delighted and told me of others who have done the same.

She walked me around the property and across neighbor's lawns, pointing out what had been moved or changed and also what was the same. She shared memories of her Dad and those days. She asked again what years I was here and figured she should have remembered the family name, which she didn't.

I took pictures and asked what happened to the swamp. She recalled her brothers going over there to shoot frogs, which is just what we did. She gave me her name (it was Clare) and encouraged me to call or write if I had any questions. When I got home I sent her a note of thanks with some photos.

I drove up the road and along the west side of the big lake stopping at the only remaining cottages. I spoke to the owner, a fellow in his 80's who has been here since the early 1950's, his wife running the place until she passed a few years ago. Now his son is taking over.

He had a dental practice just north of here and came on weekends. He told me of her rules about families: one family to a house, only full week stays and no TVs. There were boats and canoes, kayaks and swim platforms, volley ball and tether ball, basketball and room for a pickup game of whiffle ball. Kids were to play, not be entertained.

I fell in love with the guy and the place. I left promising to bring my grandchildren.

I was near Harriman before it dawned on me that they would need to bring their DVD players.

Tom

PS – I drove back down route 22 to 84. It was a trip through pre suburban America. I highly recommend it if you want to see what rural life and town centers were like in those days.

Letters to Mack

Chapter Twelve

Twin Ponds

2008

Mack,

North Pond, west side near the culvert. Cold, grey March day. Standing in my business suit and shoes, wrapped in a rain coat. Watching some bubbles, wishing they were rising insects. Noticed a small white thing on the water. Figured it was a feather left from some grooming drake. Took my eye off it for a minute and a huge splash called my attention to it again – but it was gone.

Then the strangest thing happened. A fish, a huge fish, came up almost all the way out of the water, 2/3rds at least, to gulp something down. I cursed that I didn't have a camera then I remembered my cell phone. I took it out and before I could set it up he came again, and again, and again. Five times up and down, one right after the other, each time slamming back into the water like a whale rather than turning and re-entering like a salmon.

I saw him but my eyes were playing tricks. I thought he had a head like a trout, but he was too big. I though he had sides like a rainbow, but how could it be? He must be a carp because he certainly did not look like a bass. But was he?

I waited over 30 minutes with my camera ready on video mode. I missed a single jump. I walked to the other side of the pond, explored the stream and came back to the water's edge. He came again. This time he was preceded by what looked like four large bubbles, or were they more of those white feather-like things? After they appeared so did he.

I walked back to the side I started on and waited, camera ready. I could see his wake as he moved under the surface, to the right, then to the left, more bubbles and a rise but just barely breaking the surface this time.

I told myself I had to go. It was cold and almost noon. I waited for the whistles to blow, ran 20 seconds of video hoping to, by chance, catch the next rise, then forced myself to head to the car.

Twin Ponds, where we rode our bikes and caught sunnies as kids. Remember?

Tom

Chapter Thirteen

Shared Waters

2008

Mack,

Work has always found a way to compliment my need to fish. Even when it seems to be interfering, a proper attitude can turn it into a platform instead of a barricade. I had to be in Albany on May 5th, a Tuesday. Four hour trip each way and my leg not tolerating time in the car well. An old hamstring injury seems to be reasserting itself making any seat uncomfortable. Needless to say, I was not looking forward to the trip. One way to make it less painful was to add two days of fishing to the itinerary. The pain would still be there but I wouldn't care about it as much.

Roscoe was the first stop. I arrived at noon after a late
start due to another dog incident the night before. Otto had
swallowed yet another indigestible item and was in pain as
we were going to bed. The panic mentality of past bloats
took hold and Sue was urging me to take him to the
animal ER. I resisted having just paid a small fortune to
remove his last gastronomic adventure. I took him outside,
where animals want to be when in pain, and bedded down
on the deck with him. By 2 AM he apparently passed the
item or the gas it caused and was looking to play catch.
Anyway, I got a late start.

The river was low and clear and the weather overcast but
not raining. The weekend crowds were still on the river
but would thin out as they needed to head home so I didn't
avoid the crowded parking lot at Barnhart's. I walked in
prepared to stay until dark and hoped for a hatch. The
water was cold and the reports not too encouraging, but
you never know when it is going to break open. I entered
the stream straight from the parking lot and was flanked
by others, but at a good distance.

One young fellow was snapping his leader just
downstream of me and I was tempted to go over and help
him out when his buddy came along and made some
adjustments to his casting. Later we exchanged hellos and
he confided that it was his first time and he had not caught
anything yet. I assured him he was in good company. He
mentioned that it was his Dad's gear and that he was more
experienced having fished the Henry's Fork of the Snake
and all. I smiled and wished him good day.

I wait for the rises and for the bugs. There were several spin fishermen around which I had noticed the year before as well, more than in previous years. I have nothing against the spinning rod and own several. It's just fly fishing country and it seems out of place. Perhaps on Junction Pool it would be alright, but at Barnhart's? They were far enough away not to interfere with "my water" so I let the thoughts pass.

After several hours of fly changes and double rigged droppers, a few leader snarls and some healthy meditation, I moved downstream to Hendricksons Pool which, as I predicted, was now empty of its weekend visitors. I like to fish it from the far bank, not the road side, but the wading across can be difficult this time of year. I pick up a stick to balance with and make it over without incident.

I worked the seams at the head of the pool, coming off the riffle, where the large back eddy pushes the water out toward the other side. First fishing in close and then exploring out further.

I had a compara dun style fly I had picked up at Caucci's place last year. He swears by his secret dubbing formula and I cannot argue with him as it has worked so well that I only had one of the flies left. I fish it from April to June and it works. It is darker than the classic Hendrickson and smaller than the Iso, but it works.

So I launch a cast to the far seam and it sits right on the edge moving slowly, so slowly that I am tempted to pick it up when a pair of lips smack it. I am, as usual after a long dry spell, startled and fail to properly set the hook. After a brief encounter he is off but I am juiced.

I try upstream of the spot, in toward the bank, and then try to lay it where he last was. It was either him again or his brother who took it, and I was ready: a feisty brown in the net. I reset and explored the area picking another up a little downstream and a third on a bad cast that landed far short of its intended goal, but I let it fish through. I was in heaven. I then had two misses and when I looked up, I was no longer alone.

Three fellows, apparently a father and two adult sons, had entered the riffle above and were moving to cover the entire head of the pool in a kind of a half circle, like they were working a seine together. They had spinning rods and plastic shopping bags tucked into their belts as a kind of soft tackle box. They proceeded to flip their lures throughout the pool spanning from the head where they stood to well past where I was working the water. I was incredulous.

They were conversing in their native tongue and I gave them the benefit of the doubt that they were not trying to be invasive. They smiled pleasantly, even asking me how many I had caught, as they moved even closer. I fought the tendency to associate their choice of tackle with their stream ethics. I repressed the "they are not of this country, therefore not good people" bias all too common today. Son of an immigrant, I try to be generous with those who are new to our country, our ways, our laws, so why not our fishing?

Maybe they would have been receptive to some tips and a mild lesson in stream courtesy. Maybe they just didn't know.

I wanted to shout: "No morte" hoping the Latin would transcend whatever European culture they were from when one caught a fish and stealth-fully put it in his plastic bag, stashing it up on the bank.

My blood pressure is already too high and I have a way of escalating from a kind word to a major lecture (or worse) all too easily. I tried to continue but soon lost my concentration, hooking the overhanging tree a few times. I chose to go back upstream rather than deal with it. It was better to leave for everyone's sake, except the fish's.

I later met some fellows in the parking lot gearing down who mentioned that a car just pulled out and threw all their trash on the ground, pointing in disgust to the pile. I told them my story and they said in unison:

"That was them."

Trash? Who does that anymore? Who litters? Not knowing stream courtesy is one thing but littering? I can still see that American Indian in the ad with the tear in his eye.

The trash was cleaned up and the day put behind me as I headed for the motel, but the thought kept running through my head:

133

"Trash?"

Tom

Chapter Fourteen

Missoula to Yellowstone by way of the Big Hole

2008

Hey Mack,

Jerry and I went to the fly fishing show in Somerset NJ last January, not sure we would be able to manage a trip away this summer. With his practice rebuilding and me without a job, we were afraid to make a commitment. On the other hand we both have wanted to go to Labrador and fish for giant brookies. There were no fewer than 6 booths with outfitters who were anxious to take us there. We talked to each one and slowly the enthusiasm subsided as we figured out that the choices were early season (July) fishing with lots of biting insects or late season (August) fishing with few biting fish. Then there was the small matter of cost. The average was $6000 each for a short week – plus airfare.

We wandered down the aisle to the guy from Chile with the girl friend by his side. He was in full sales mode and the photos showed guys in heavy coats fishing big water from boats. No thanks. Then we came across a great deal: multiple Montana float trips packaged with most expenses included, and at a good price. We took the brochure not certain of what we were going to do.

A few weeks later, on the way to a TU meeting, we talked it over. How good a deal was it? What was the catch? Were they going to put us in flea bag motels or shorten the fishing day for such a good price? I called the outfitter and he gave me the names of the motels – respectable Comfort Inn types. He said they would start early and fish until dark. Then he threw in that he was reducing the cost by $200 if we signed up this week. I went back to Jerry and we decided to take a chance. 5 days, four floats on three rivers – The Bitterroot, the Big Hole and the Beaverhead. All guides, transportation and hotels included. One more logistical problem to solve: We wanted to go to West Yellowstone for 3 days at the end of our trip to meet up with the other guys from Long Island. We would need a rental car and the town we were ending up in, Dillon, has no car agencies.

> "Not a problem" said he, "I'll drive you to Butte Airport where they are sure to have cars."

It was a done deal.

We prepared for the trip by downsizing our packing and selecting only those flies we would need. Jerry did a much better job than I did but we still ended up paying the fee for checking an extra bag each. We didn't want to drag luggage through the airport when we changed in Salt Lake since we usually get two gates that are at least a mile apart. We went to the red cap at LGA and he said it would be $50. Jerry handed him cash and he said he would be right back. He came back with great news – he had the fees waived for the extra bags, grasping the $50 tightly in his hand as he put the claim tags on our bags. Jerry got his $50 back and gave him a $20. Had we paid with a credit card waiving fees would not have been an option, I am sure.

Our flights were early and our luggage was among the first off the plane in Missoula. We were standing outside looking for our ride when an attractive woman came up and introduced herself. She was the outfitter's wife. We were off. When we got to town, we asked her about fishing that night. She offered to pick us up later and bring us to a good spot. This was turning out better than we could have hoped for. That evening she picked us up at 6:30 and drove us just north of the old bridge. We saw lots of rises but did not connect. The trip was underway.

At 8:30, after breakfast just a few doors down at Perkins, we met Wes, our guide for the day. Wes was a native from Darby. He smoked small hand rolled cigarettes that looked like joints. We put in at Wally Crawford and started with a dry and a dropper. He seemed pleased that we knew how to cast and mend, all from the seat of a rubber raft. I hit a few white fish (large ones) and then our first trout. The day continued well for me but Jerry had a dry spell. Wes had him with double dries most of the day and finally switched him to a hopper and a dropper in the late afternoon.

We got out and waded periodically and he had a few special spots with special fish. One was by a tall pine where a large brown sat at the bottom of a pool which was also filled with "cutts" which were feasting on gray drakes that were falling out of the tree. Jerry went for him first and after a rest, I gave him a try but we had to be satisfied with the smaller fish who aggressively took what we offered.

Another spot was by a side channel with a large pile of tangled roots and tree trunks. Wes climbed on it and spotted some nice fish on the far side. I was to wade across the channel and position myself to flip a fly at them. I had seen a rise in the path where he wanted me to cross and so I fished it first landing a nice cutthroat. Jerry then came with me and worked the other fish but they were not to be moved.

We had been picked up at 8:30 and were on the river by 9 or so. We stopped for lunch at 4 PM. Could this be the half way mark of the float? Jerry and I were already tired and told Wes to move along as fast as he'd like. There were a number of diversion dams to facilitate the siphoning off of irrigation water, each forming a small waterfall. We rode over the first but had to portage the next 4. Wes took the raft through them as we walked. In retrospect, I would opt to ride through them next time. We didn't get out until dark, as promised. It was a good day on a great river. I'd

138

go back again and spend a few days exploring more of it including its branches at the head waters.

Pizza Hut was our choice for dinner. No comment. We had a good breakfast at Perkins the next morning and were introduced to Jeff who was to be our guide for the next three days. We drove over to Darby, stopped at the fly shop (there only is one) and geared up. It's a nice little town and if I come again I would stay down here and fish the upper Bitterroot.

As we came over the rise, following the path of Chief Joseph's March, the Big Hole Valley opened up to us. I could envision a million head of cattle and cow pokes in chaps. The river meanders through it with a very low gradient and soft flow for most of its journey. As we drove north and east (I think) the river began to run closer to the hills and trees lined its bank. We put it at Divide. It was almost like a canyon as the valley had narrowed and the river was in a rock strewn rush to get where it was going.

Wes had mentioned that the next rafts were going to be small. Meanwhile, we thought his was not too roomy. Turned out to be true: very simple and basic raft with an aluminum frame resting on it and two seats, fore and aft. The guide sat on a cooler and rowed. The floor was rubber so you couldn't stand even if you wanted to. Casting from a sitting position all day made me feel a little confined, but it is what it is when you go on these adventures. No sense getting riled up about it.

So we start off on the Big Hole with hoppers and droppers and Jerry hooks up right away picking a nice fish out of a big boulder pillow. We get excited and I wait for the guide to drop the anchor, the normal procedure when fighting a fish from a boat. Instead he is rowing like mad to get us to shore in a wide, wild river full of rocks. I watch as we pass all kinds of good looking water and pockets. I look down to find the anchor line and it's not there. There is no anchor. Holy cow, what kind of a deal is this? Every time we change flies or catch fish we have to row to shore to secure the raft, accumulatively passing by miles of fish.

"No anchor?"

Once we got Jerry's fish released I asked him why no anchor? His reply was when he gets his own raft it WILL have an anchor. Later I pursued the questioning further, ever curious as to why someone would not have an anchor, a primary tool and safety feature on boats at home. He said that the outfitter knew someone whose anchor got stuck in a rock during a heavy flow and it stretched and flipped the craft. Lives were lost. So no anchors. Holy cow.

The river changed from a rocky rush to a meandering flow as we headed toward Melrose. The fishing slowed for me but Jerry continued to connect. I had a good day on the Bitterroot so I guess it was just one of those days. I kept working the banks, looking for a big brown with the hopper sans dropper, ever hopeful. As we were almost done for the day, I finally connected and she was a beauty worth the wait.

By the time we got to town all the restaurants worth going to were closed. It was looking like Mickey D's or Pizza Hut, (not again), when Jeff drove by this white school bus with lights on and a sign painted on the side: Tacos. Served by a momma with child who didn't seem to speak the language but smiled and filled our plates with tasty fare that more than filled our empty bellies. It was great.

We started on the Beaverhead at the foot of the Clark Dam. We parked the raft near the highway over pass and walked upstream toward the dam. There were a ton of people along the way and some were catching fish. The terminal tackle was like a black fish rig at home with a bobber on it: two nymphs with a chunk of lead on the bottom. The set up was a bitch to cast, like hauling egg sinkers on a light weigh spinner. Jerry went up and I went in by the bridge and worked up toward him. I hit a white fish first but as I got better at the technique, watching the drag but also letting it drift in the currents, a few good browns came in.

We heard a rumble in the distance and the horizon, or what we could see of it since we were sort of in the valley of the foot hills, was turning dark. One by one the other fisherpersons packed it in as the wind picked up and the sky grew darker. The fish kept biting. A few drops of rain and some more wind, we headed for the raft and our rain jackets. The rain came harder, the sky now midnight dark with the only light coming from the edge where you could still see brilliant blue. Lightning was popping, no, crashing, all around us. We laid our graphite lightning rods in the raft and headed for the under pass. The rain felt like bullets hitting our backs. The temperatures dropped from the 80's to the 60's to the 40's in 15 minutes. We climbed up to the top of the underpass, like they tell you to do in tornados, although we did not see any funnels. It was cold and uncomfortable but out of the wind and rain. I looked for some timber to build a fire but the cement was bare of flammable debris. The rain came through the bridge portals in water falls that would give Victoria's a run for her money. In about 45 minutes it passed and left only a light rain and the cold temperatures behind. We climbed back out on to the river, and still caught fish.

I hated to leave but we had a 5 hour float ahead of us. We nosed the raft downstream and navigated what seemed to be a narrow canal. Using the same rig, but not having to cast, we had fish on every few feet it seemed. Some were small but most were of good size, although no monsters. This kept up until we came to the first irrigation diversion dam. A bump in the water as we cleared it with lines reeled in. After that, the action slowed as the day cooled even more. We had every piece of clothing on that we had plus the life jackets to try and get warm. We fished a small island without much luck and then floated the beaver meadow-like twists and turns with a fish every now and again, but nowhere near the action of the top. We pulled in at dark and were glad to be heading for a hot shower.

We started the next day at Organ Pipes, again on the Beaverhead. Here the stream meanders even more than above. In fact, after a few hours of fishing and drifting, we could still look up and see the namesake rocks. It was more crowded than the day before, probably because there wasn't a 60 mile an hour gale blowing through. Fish were selective. We had some hits, including one I got out of the raft for. I crawled up to a back water where a small creek joined the river. It was a big swirling pool – 50 feet across with several different currents cutting across and through it. I had what I thought was a good drift from the far side, up the back eddy and across the middle. I made the same cast several times. At the end of the drift the Adams sank and I let it work its way back into the main current.

Another cast in the same spot and just as it was about to be taken by the main river current he hit. Nice cutt. Jerry hooked a good one on a dry, also while out of the raft. By the way, there were very few places where you could get out. The final fish of the day was a big one just before the take out and Jerry was playing him well when I messed up the netting as the guide held the boat to the steep rock bank. I felt terrible. We saw the fish and it was a beauty.

This was our last day in Dillon. We were supposed to drive to Butte before dinner and so we got off the river at 4 PM instead of 8 or 9. When we got back to the motel we had a message that we were to stay another night. We had motel reservations in Butte and were expected in West Yellowstone the next morning. We made the adjustment but when we met the outfitter the next morning he wanted us to have a leisurely breakfast with him and his other sports after which we could mosey up to Butte. We said no way. Our plans had already been altered without asking us and we needed to be at the car rental agency as early as possible. There were some hard feelings, I think, but he got us up there on time.

We picked up the car at the airport and one of the tires was low on air. After the bad alternator the year before, we were not taking any chances. They sent us to the tire shop in town as there were no other cars to give us. They checked them over, found no problem, and we were off to West Yellowstone. We stopped in Ennis for lunch and had that outrageous strawberry pie again. It was early afternoon when we checked into the Lazy G.

We met up with Jay, Pete and Pete, who were staying at a frontier town type accommodation, (which was nice but a little too Disney), and compared stories of the early part of the week. Then Peter, Rick and Tommy showed up. We briefly discussed plans for the evening: Peter, Tommy and Rick went to the Madison while the rest of us decided to do the Firehole in the Park.

We headed for Biscuit Basin where the stream leaves its smoking, steamy upstream waters and meanders into a wide meadow which seemed to go as far as the eye could see. It was channel-like but zig-zaggy with trout rising throughout its course. The bank was a few feet high and you could walk the edge fishing across the narrow stream. Once hooked up it was a job to get down into the stream (and back out) but most were small enough to be hoisted and released. Jerry was one of the first with a fish on and Jay marveled how he leapt into the stream with no concern for his safety. What a man. He later shared that he did not feel as manly as he crawled out on all fours.

This was one of the most picturesque scenes of the trip with the sun setting over this grassy meadow. I followed it downstream as far as made sense, given the hour, and there were rising fish at every bend. I fished to them all with little success. Whether it was the fly or the inability to get a good drag free drift, I don't know, but I kept trying. Finally on the way back a little guy did me the favor of taking my offering and all was right with the world.

There is nothing better than breakfast at the Black Bear Pancake House with the boys while we plan our day: Consensus was to fish the Madison and Gibbon inside the Park with a dinner at Eino's. It was Jay and the two Pete's with Jerry and me. The others headed for the Madison below Quake Lake to meet up with Jeff and Scott. We traveled up to the big meadow on the Gibbon, well above the falls, and tried the gin clear water that wound through the meadow that seems to reach to the far mountains. There were fish for sure, but spooky, and with all the tourist activity around compounded by a high hot sun, fishing was limited. I walked a bit, found some log jams and other cover and spooked a few but nothing to the net. Beautiful as it was, we decided to work our way back.

We hop-scotched each other, stopping at different turn-outs and chatting on the radios back and forth. At one point I was on the Madison crossing the slippery rocks to the far side when I heard Jerry talking on the radio. He had picked up chatter from some kids and not having his hearing aid, which we left in Dillon, he was talking back

145

to them as if it was me. I kept trying to tell him what was going on but it was clear that I was not getting through to him as he yelled into the device. It was, however, very clear to the guys down the river who got the biggest kick out of our antics. We ended up way downstream working some water which certainly would be wonderful about 7 that evening, but with agreed to dinner plans for 6, we packed it in and headed for home.

Eino's is the bar/restaurant where you can buy a raw steak and cook it yourself. The fun is its uniqueness more than the joy of cooking. We all ate well and they do have a great green salad. Like the trout that won't come out until dark, I wonder what it would be like in the bar here closer to closing time – with all the interesting undergarments hanging from the ceiling, I am sure it would be an entertaining place to be when they are "rising." After dinner I took Jerry over to Grayling Creek but it was a frustrating time for both of us with low water and slippery wading. We were just doing a bit too much. We lasted an hour and went to town for an ice cream cone and then to bed.

Saturday, our last day, came too fast. We made plans to drive through the north portion of the Park and fish Slough Creek after which Jerry and I would head for the airport motel and a morning flight. The drive was amazing with vast vistas of undisturbed wilderness and millions of wild flowers, more than I had ever seen on my previous trips to these or any other mountains. Aided by a healthy snow pack and some rain, the flowers were everywhere. We crossed the Lamar River which was still running cloudy and made the turn to Slough. The long dirt road with the predictable dust had a wilderness feel to it, but at the terminus there was a small, neat camp ground with tents and trailers (no generators, thank God) and a beautiful river loaded with modest sized trout that were eager for the fly. Grey Drakes or anything close kept you in the action.

Peter and I went upstream passing the "Don't Pass This Point – Bear Country" sign and found some interesting water with deep pools. I asked Peter about the "Meadows" and he said they were miles upstream and we decided to leave them for another time, perhaps with a guide who knew how to deal with the hike and the bears. Later we joined the others downstream as a returning pack train of riders came by, each with his canister of bear spray at the ready.

It was time to go. One by one we left the water and broke down our rods, Jerry and I putting them away for good as this was our exit. Warm handshakes and hugs with promises to do it all again next year. Our ride to Bozeman paralleled the Yellowstone for miles which, although well used by rafters and fishermen, did not have the appeal of the beauty we had just left.

That night Jerry asked:

>"If there was anything you could change about this trip, what would it be?"

>"An anchor on the Big Hole" I quickly said.

147

"Agreed" he replied.

Tom

Chapter Fifteen

Montauk on a Fly

2008

Mack,

Montauk in October is nirvana but I had an opportunity to share a charter with a friend who had a reservation in September. The guide assured him it would be a great time to go, as long as the hurricanes stayed away.

Last year we tried but ended up heading back to bed after an early morning call that the seas were unfishable due to storms. That day Paul made the reservation for September 24, a year ago. Guides, the good ones, tend to be booked in this season.

I was up at 3 AM and headed out East to meet Paul and Robin our guide, (www.longislandflyfishing.com), at the West Lake Town Ramp. I pulled into town at 5:30 and Mr. John's Pancakes wasn't even stirring yet. I went to the deli across from Gossman's Dock that caters to fisherman and other early risers for some breakfast. Before I could wolf down my egg sandwich the cell phone rang. It was Paul. He was at the Exxon in town.

We arrived at the dock followed shortly by Robin and his 23 foot center console with a large Yamaha four stroke. Amazing how quiet it ran. He said he can leave it on as he approaches a school of fish without disturbing them. With wind and a 6 foot swell predicted, I was thinking he won't have to worry about sneaking up on any schools today. Temperatures were forecasted to be in the high 60's but I dressed warm none the less knowing the ocean can be cool – and wet – regardless of the weatherman. Long-johns, fishing shirt, thermal vest, sweat shirt all covered by my rain jacket. I had a cut off pair of boot foot waders with my yellow and blue fishing boots from E&B Marine. (Are they still around?) I figured I could shed items as the day warmed but as we headed back in at 4 that afternoon, I had taken nothing off.

We headed out of the inlet and immediately hit nasty swells. Sloppy with the wind from north east and the tide running from the south. The boat had a Vee up front but still took some jaw jarring pounding. As we got out by the lighthouse it was worse and I was wondering how the hell we were going to fish this slop. As we came around the

point toward Turtle Bay, we were in the lee of the land
and it seemed to settle down.

I brought my 9 foot 9 weight rod with an intermediate
sinking line. Paul brought two, one similar to mine and
one with a full sinking line. That one never left the holster.
Robin also had some spinning outfits in case we couldn't
handle the fly lines in this wind. The boat was not big in
any sense. The fore deck was three tiered so that, were it a
quiet day on the back bay, one could step up to the bow
and fish like they do in the Keys. Today, no one was going
up there. In fact it was damn hard to just keep your
balance in the pit of the bow section, falling to the seat or
my knees more often than standing up straight.

The gunnels were for leaning into, especially when trying
to hook an Albie (false albacore) as you need to tuck the
rod under your arm and strip in with both hands, one after
the other, to keep the fly moving fast. This was almost
impossible to do without falling. Meanwhile the fly line is
all over the deck and as we rocked, I continually stepped
on it or leaned against the gunnels with the line in
between.

The aft section was no better except you could position
yourself in the corner and lean into the back of the helm
bench, bracing each foot, one on the stern and the other
either port or starboard, depending on which side you
were fishing. This was as good as it got.

The technique out here is simple: cast, even a modest cast
will do as long as it is straight. Then, and this is important,

point the rod tip toward the fly, followed by the stripping. If you don't point at the fly, the strip merely moves the rod tip and not the fly. I thought Robin was going to clock me one until I finally got it.

The boat was usually positioned so that we could cast with the wind. When it was in our face, because a school suddenly came up on the opposite side, even a cast well loaded and aimed often fell in a pile of loops alongside the boat. Rather than trying to figure out the "into the wind" cast, I just went with it and passed up the windward fish. Luckily for us, there were plenty on both sides most of the time.

We get settled off Turtle Bay, just outside the casting range of all the surfcasters on the beach, and a school of Albies, with hundreds of birds working over them, appears. My first cast was successful – in hooking a seagull. They were so thick it was inevitable. My next cast went well enough but I was having difficulty with the pointing and stripping. The boat was in the surf and a tidal drift so even if I pointed my tip toward the fly it wasn't long before the line was at right angles to the tip.

Paul hooked up first and the fish tore off line and went immediately into his backing. I went to pull my line in so he could work his fish and in so doing hooked up as well. Line flying off the huge reel with knuckles being bashed by the spinning handle, and into my backing.

Paul brought his to the boat as I continued to fight mine. Keep in mind this is a fly rod with a fine tapered tip and no butt section to speak of. The fish has all the leverage. He finally tired out enough so I could bring him to the boat and a fine Albie he was. The three of us were laughing and slapping each other and going on how unbelievable it was, first few casts and two terrific fish. There are days when that just doesn't happen, as you well know.

As we celebrated, the pod moved toward the beach and the surf casters, the rocks and the breaking waves. Did I mention the 6 foot swell? We reset ourselves and went in after them. Robin had to nose the boat into the waves to prevent being side swiped (you know what that's like) and we had to deal with the wind. We hooked up again and then they moved back outside.

We hooked, lost and landed a bunch more when a red hew appeared in the water. It was from anchovies, I think, and they were being devoured by bass. There were dozens of them of all sizes smashing this little bait fish. The first one in was small, maybe 26 inches. The rest were bigger. The largest of the day was one I caught using a different technique. Instead of stripping the fly in, I let it settle in the midst of the pod and then twitched it after it sank. He was 34 inches and 16 pounds.

There were blue fish mixed in as well and Robin kept saying:

"Fish to the ones with the stripes."

No kidding Karnack, but how? The blues would grab the fly and because they were tied with circle hooks which lodge in the lip, the line didn't break off, at least not right away. Big blues. Powerful. Running off the reel and fighting like you know they can. I must have lost 10 or 15 flies to them while landing my share.

You know how a blue can look like a torpedo shooting through a school of bunker? Maybe the surge creates a splashy wake 4 -5 feet long? Well we saw something do that only it created a torpedo-like wake about 50 feet long. Robin said it was probably a blue fin tuna.

I don't know how many fish we hooked and boated but there were more than we could physically handle. At one point Paul and I were sitting, just looking at all these fish surrounding the boat. My legs and knees were banged up, muscles sore, my hands raw from all the stripping and slamming and reeling. It is almost a week later and they are still sore. The seas were treacherous and thrilling. It felt so good to be alive out there. I never gave a thought to the danger involved, much as we didn't that night in the Gut. It was exhilarating. Robin later mentioned that about three boats a year are capsized in surf like this.

At 3:30 we headed for Shagwong (north side of the light). The seas were still sloppy but smaller. There were birds working a spread out school and we edged the boat to the front of it. Two casts and we had to move again. I was determined to get a hook up and worked my butt off to do so missing two hits due to adrenaline, tugging too hard.

Finally I had one on and he gave us a good run but turned out to be another blue.

Robin, being the good guide that he is, promised a full day meaning until dark and we had left the dock about 6:45 AM. We next headed for the back side of the jetty, which protects the inlet, to do some calm water casting. Paul and I looked at each other and told Robin to head in. We had had the day of our lives and it was time.

I look at the photos and can feel the boat rocking, the fish surging and the soul of the salt water filling my bones.

Tom

Letters to Mack

Chapter Sixteen

Jerry

December 5, 2009

Mack,

A eulogy:

I was working on a project in my garage with the door open and Jerry was exercising by walking around the block each night. He came up to see what I was doing. It was a wooden strip canoe and he really got excited as he loved things traditional, outdoor and wooden. We began to talk fishing and he invited me to go with him during the upcoming spring to the Beaverkill for a day. In my experience, a trip to the Catskills was a weeklong excursion. I was a bit taken aback thinking of doing it in one day but said yes.

The day came and we left early and came home late. I had a great time and was in awe of his fly fishing knowledge, experience and skill. He knew all the pools by name, (before they put up signs). He could tell you the history behind each and how it came to be named. He knew where to place the fly and how to fish it. He knew which fly to use, and could give you its name in English or Latin. He was not condescending about it nor was he impatient with my flailing away, as he landed fish after fish.

We made arrangements to do it again before we hit the driveway. That was the beginning of a long and wonderful relationship that spanned three decades and covered so much more than fishing.

I am not much of a conversationalist, so early on I let him know that I am okay with quiet car rides. We were reminiscing the other day and he reminded me of that with a smile, as over the years we talked of so many things.

He was not a hugger, at least not with the guys, but he was warm and giving, especially to those who needed help. I suppose it was this trait, along with his intelligence, that made him such a good physician. He knew his patients and was a gifted diagnostician. Charles Neuner tells the story of being sick upstate and going to the hospital where no one could figure out what was wrong. He had them call Jerry and after a few questions he told them to check for a particular ailment and that was it. He was my doctor for the last 25 years and I know I will never have another like him.

He was a great poker player. Early in our time together we went to Cranberry Lake to fish the Oswagachie and there was a deck of cards in the house we rented. I asked him if he wanted to play. He said:

"You don't want to play cards with me."

I pushed him and he quickly dispatched me in a game of gin rummy.

He would call me and say:

"I played cards Tuesday."

Then he would wait for me to ask:

"How did you do?"

The answer was always the same. His mind worked in such a way that he had an advantage over the others, but if you want to know his real secret, here it is: he only played hands that looked like they could win. He made contributions back to the group as well, but loved the game probably as much as he loved to fish and work. But family was his first love.

He treasured each of his kids. He would regale me with stories of their adventures and accomplishments, grandkids and spouses, as well as his two brothers and their families. I know each of them although some I have never met. I had the pleasure of traveling with the three brothers to the San Juan River.

As the formalities wore off and the personalities emerged they became three kids in Brooklyn, jabbing at each other in the back seat, playing the license plate game on the interstate and telling of how they convinced Barry that it was Spain he could see across the water from their Manhattan Beach home.

He adored his wife. One time when we were having a discussion around the limited time we have to fish I asked him:

> "Why did you get remarried when you could have been free to travel and fish whenever and wherever you wanted?"

He had a simple reply:

> "I fell in love."

He was very open about his devotion and love for her. They truly had something very special between them.

We shared political views and talked of current events and work. He would tell me of some journal article he read or a situation in the practice. I would share my sales stories with him and my ongoing struggle to fit into organizational life. We were each proud of the other's accomplishments and hurt for the other when times were bad. When his partners decided to sell the practice, he summoned the strength to start over again. I was in awe.

During that time I would ask him why not just retire and relax. He said:

"And what would I do?"

He needed to be not just busy but vital. He needed to practice what he did so well. He needed to take care of his patients, many who have been going to him since they were children.

We were at lunch in Roscoe when he got the call from his lawyer that he could open up in the next town and he was elated. There was no need to talk of retirement. He said he would retire two days after he died. Indeed I saw him in his office on November 13th and he was taking calls from patients up until a week ago at home.

I could go on for hours about our adventures and about all the people whose lives he touched. How he was generous and kind, while having opinions and a mild stubborn streak. How he would rather go to the dentist than listen to a Yankee game. How he was one of the first to donate to the Catskill Fly Fishing Center. How he gave his antique Leonard rod to Trout Unlimited to auction off.

I have been fortunate to share many hours with him on rivers from New York to Montana to New Mexico. We fished from Long Island to Pennsylvania to the Adirondacks, but the place he loved the most was the Beaverkill, the Catskills.

Last April, as he was being held captive to some infection in the hospital, he was having difficulty getting up and walking. He confided that he was worried that he would not be walking again if this continued. I suggested he visualize some place that he really wanted to walk to, hoping that it would help him get his legs moving. We looked at each other and said simultaneously:

"Barnhart's."

It is a pool on the Beaverkill that requires a walk of several hundred yards to reach the river.

In June he made that walk.

He was an amazing man and I am so fortunate to have had him as my friend.

He will be missed.

Tom

Dr. Jerome Greenholz: 12/13/1928 - 12/3/2009

Chapter Seventeen

Negley Farson

2010

Mack,

It was a few days into his final illness. He was still mentally sharp but had difficulty speaking. He sat in the chair in the middle room, holding court for his friends and family. People were coming by who had heard. His sister in law was there for the duration to support them all.

I had promised to get his books organized and to contact the various booksellers he knew of to see if they would be interested in buying the collection. He seemed to know that these books, these friends of his, would not be serving their purpose if they were to stay in the non-fishing household that was to follow.

He had me call one friend that he had lent the beautiful
Bates book on salmon to. He wanted that returned.
Interesting that he, at the same time, was telling visitors to
go look at the library and take what they like. None
complied, feeling awkward. He asked me repeatedly to
take some books but it was too soon and too hard.

I would come and sit a few hours most days. Have a cup
of tea. At first they made me coffee as they knew it was
my drink of choice, but it was a tea household and I soon
looked forward to a refreshing cup.

Jerry strained to tell me something. I listened closer:

     "Negley" he said.

     "Negley?" I repeated.

He nodded:

     "Farson" he added.

     "Negley Farson?" I said.

He nodded. He cleared his throat:

     "A book" he said.

I nodded.

     "On the right side, middle shelf."

He waved his hand in that dismissive way, when one wants someone to scoot.

I went to the library room to locate it.

The books were in some order but not one that made sense to anyone but Jerry. He periodically would go through and reorganize them, putting the old ones at the top one time and perhaps separating the English from the Americans another. I looked and looked and finally came across it, right where he said it would be.

It is a thin green book unadorned on the cover of cloth with no dust jacket. The title was *Going Fishing* and I brought it to him:

"Good writer" he said.

I flipped the pages and saw the pen and ink drawings and the chapter titles.

"Okay" I replied.

I set it aside, later returning it to its place. He slipped into a nonverbal state shortly after that and finally succumbed.

Sometime later, I continued to catalogue the books in a spread sheet and put them in order by author and year, numbering each to make finding them for their final distribution easier. I came to Negley Farson and promised myself to read it before it left. I told his wife that I was borrowing it a few weeks ago and she, like Jerry, said:

"Keep it."

That was not my intent. I wanted to see if there was some message in it that Jerry intended me to get. It was published in 1947 and the stories are of his travels around the world and trout fishing prior to the Second World War.

As much as I enjoy books, I am a slow reader. I also tend to read the whole book including introductions and notes. This book opens with a statement:

"This is just a story of some rods, and the places they take you to."

About mid page it states:

"I love rods, I suppose... I love using them. But, if I can't, I can get a lot of fun by just taking them out of their cases and looking at them."

The page ends:

"But chiefly I love rods because of their associations, the places they have brought me to... This magic wand has revealed to me some of the loveliest places on earth."

I read the rest of the book which was interesting and entertaining. This English newspaper man and author had a life no modern man could possibly aspire to, the good old days as they are often called. Upon finishing it this morning I went back and read the statement at the beginning. It was then that I knew what it was Jerry was trying to tell me.

Enjoy your rods, and your kit. Enjoy recollecting all those amazing times that we had.

His wife, on an earlier occasion, shared with me that Jerry was really a very demanding and exacting person. Few people pleased him as he expected perfection. Vacations were often critiqued upon return as well as while en route. She went on to say:

> "But he never once complained about your trips together. Not once. Fish or no fish. Good weather or bad, he would smile and say it was great."

As I sit here going through my tackle, preparing for the coming season, shaking off the cabin fever as the snow remains on the lawn, I think about where this gear has taken me, the friends it has introduced me to, and how good all those fishing trips were.

And they were, every one.

Tom

Going Fishing by Negley Farson, published by Harcourt, Brace and Company 1947

Letters to Mack

Chapter Eighteen

Adirondack Reprieve

2010

Mack,

Besides the June club trip and two short trips to the Beaverkill, one each to the Carmans and the Nissequogue, my trout fishing has been limited this season. I needed some more. As you know, I like to go up to the Adirondacks at least once each year for some hiking and fishing on the Ausable.

I am still not ready to do a peak, continuing to heal from the cancer therapy more than the cancer. I feel pretty good and figure I could take a level hike along with some time on the river. There is something about the mountains, and especially the high peaks, that help to heal and refresh. It will do me good, I rationalize.

I wanted to stay near the river rather than in Keene Valley where I usually stay. No sense driving back and forth since I won't be hiking any peaks from the Garden anyway. I consider a few untested B&B's in the Wilmington area and decide to go with a friend's suggestion and try the Wilderness Inn. Turned out to be reasonably priced and cabins rather than a strip-mall-type motel. There is also a restaurant attached for dinner, although it is closed on Wednesdays.

I drove up early Tuesday and had the windows open to the 90 degree heat. I averaged 32 miles per gallon on the way up. Coming down I used the air and averaged 28. I was thinking about how the windows open should create drag and cause more gas to be burned but I guess the a/c is worse or my driving damn inconsistent.

The cabin was nice but a bit stuffy. I opened the windows, turned on the fan and it was fine. I took a ride up Whiteface. Since I would not be hiking, I thought I'd at least take in the view. It was worthwhile and reconnected me with that which I enjoy so much – the majesty of the mountain top and its vista. The heat had filled the air with moisture so the visibility was hazy. Giant, Dix, Noonmark, Nippletop, Marcy, all still there.

I had passed Better's shop on the way but, sadly, there were no cars out front and it was dark. On the corner of the Whiteface Highway was a new shop called the Ausable River Two Fly Shop so I stopped. Three guys were sitting inside and one was testing rods out front. They carry Hardy and Grey brands. The owner greeted me and all chimed in as to how the river was too warm and no fish to be had. I pressed them to see what the options might be and asked about the upstream Ausable as it crosses Adirondac Loj Road. Tom, the owner, thought it may also be too warm but, realizing I was familiar with the area, asked if I wanted to do some brook trout fishing.

There was a place nearby. He gave me directions and even showed me on Google Earth where it was. I thanked him and went to leave, as I really didn't need anything. He asked if I'd like to buy a hat with the fly shop logo on it. I said, uncharacteristically:

"Maybe tomorrow."

I was intent on fishing what has become my favorite spot on the Ausable where there always seemed to be fish either rising or easily tempted. I had dinner at the Wilderness Inn which was good, then headed to the stream. I fished the new Charles Neuner 6 foot, 6 inch bamboo 4 weight. It is beautifully made and I was anxious to see how it felt. I matched it to my Hardy Featherweight and tied on a Fran Better's Usual in rust color.

There were rises in the smooth water before the cascade section but the fly was not a match for some subsurface emerger they were hitting. I tied on an emerger and offered it to them a few more times, putting them down. I moved to the pocket water. There is one pool at the top of the cascade where the current flows upstream and I usually get a reaction. It did not disappoint me. I had several rises to an Adams and one small taker.

I switched to a caddis and nothing. Went back to the Adams and it worked again. I moved down to better water with confidence in the fly and the rod, which proved effective in the flats and the pockets. There is something magical about a handmade cane rod, especially when you know the maker and the quality is apparent. It casts smooth and gentle, even when laying out a significant length of line. I worked until dark and had two nice fish to my credit along with the first one which was too small to count. I headed to town for some ice cream, then a good hot shower (great water pressure) and bed.

I awoke around 5:45 and fought the urge to roll over for 40 more winks. I pulled on my clothes and headed for the same spot. One of the guys at the shop emphasized that morning was the best bet. I repeated my routine from the night before. There was a tiny trico hatch going on but I didn't want to deal with tying on size 24 flies that I could not see. I stayed with the Adams and was pleasantly surprised by a good size fish. Around 9:30 I walked out and met a fellow who was living in Queens but from western PA. We talked awhile, then I headed for the brook trout spot.

On the way, I stopped at the Dart Brook Cafe for some blueberry pancakes on the deck overlooking the motel formerly owned by my cousins, now renovated to look like an Adirondack Great Camp with twig art on the buildings and rustic chairs on the porches. I wanted to take a walk up the back to see how the vegetable garden was that once produced the most delicious potatoes and tomatoes I have ever tasted, but decided to let it be.

I followed the directions to the brook and found it without difficulty. It is a boulder filled work of art with multiple mini waterfalls and runs, pools and blow downs. I fished it downstream even though it would have been more effective, stealthier, to fish it up. The price I paid was watching several large (6-8 inch) fish scramble upon my approach but there seemed to be willing 4-5 inchers in each pocket to oblige me and my Adams.

Let me see if I can describe this properly. At one point, I was sitting high above a small pool which had a rock in the middle of its tail. The water parted and went in each direction around it and there was some depth in front. I was resting, cooling off from the 90+ degree heat, when I saw a rise on the left side of the rock. I flipped my fly. After a few casts I determined, by trial and error, how to make it float to that side, drag free. The fish came up but refused it. I repeated, as did the fish. This went on for some time before I put him down.

I backed off and sat above. I tied on some new tippet and a smaller version of the fly. After a respectable rest I went back to my casting position. Well, you really can't call it a cast, more of a flip and mend. The new fly worked and I hooked him. I was so elated that I struck him hard enough to pull the poor fellow clear out of his lie and across the pool where he quickly threw the barbless hook:

"That counts!"

I said aloud with a big smile.

As I worked my way down through amazingly beautiful settings, standing on a huge outcropping of granite worn smooth over the millenniums with a crevice for the water to travel through, I could hear the roar of a water fall. I had already traveled a distance in the hot afternoon and was drenched with sweat brought on by the constant scrambling up and down boulders, hopping and climbing. I looked toward the sound. I had to keep going to see its source.

Now all of these pockets were maybe 1 to 2 feet deep at best, hence the size of the fish. As I continued on the outcropping and crossed the flow several times to find the best footing, the sound became louder. The rock floor came to an abrupt end just ahead and beyond it the brook regained its characteristic form. In between the end of the rock and the brook was a deep, crystal clear pool big enough to swim in, maybe even dive, with water plunging into it from the rock above.

What a picture.

Tom

Chapter Nineteen

The Walk

2010

Hey Mack,

Thanksgiving 1964. You and I were 17. My family was having dinner at our house. I don't remember who was coming but whoever it was Dad did not have to drive to Westchester or the Bronx to pick them up. I know that because we took a walk that day, before dinner. It was to be the first walk we ever took, just the two of us, at least that I can recall.

We went through our backyard, along the parkway, crossed over at Old Country Road and found our way past the Jones Old Folks Home, into the fields that are now a golf course.

175

He was an outdoor person who loved hunting and fishing, camping and the woods. His high school friend, Oak, has since shared with me that the two of them studied the travels of Lewis and Clark and longed for such adventure, not that Dad was a student. We think he finished high school but we are not sure as his family imploded about that time, although no one ever talked about it.

I was brought up with *Outdoor Life* and *Field and Stream* and the Scouts. I wanted to hunt pheasants in the fields of North Dakota and catch trout in the Rockies and bass in Arkansas. I settled for fishing the Twin Ponds and hunting on the farms out east. He had bought me a 16 gauge shot gun, a Winchester Model 12 pump action, (well used and made in 1928), for my birthday the year before. As we walked we looked for signs of game: rabbit tracks and scat, birds and squirrels.

Life accelerated after that year and soon I was out of the house, in the service, and married with a child. The other day was my older son's birthday and inextricably attached to that day, which should be and is one of joy, is the fact that Dad died the same month and day, on his first birthday. The walk on Thanksgiving 1964 was our last one.

I don't recall much conversation as there never was much to begin with, both of us knowing how to socialize with others, but never gaining the gift of sharing with each other. Thoughts were few and words were fewer.

I wonder if he had a reason for that walk. Was it supposed to be a time of offering me fatherly advice, of telling me the ways of the world, of passing on the message of my heritage?

Did he want to tell me how much he wanted our relationship to be different? How he had such hopes for us and was sorry that they were not yet attained? Did he want to let me know that it was okay that I was who I had become?

I will never know.

I am not sure he had that frame of reference. I think he could barely deal with his own lost dreams.

I remember him wearing his bright red Woolrich hunting jacket and cap. It was brisk but not uncomfortable and the long walk did not tire me, although it might have him, smoker that he was. I seem to recall our coming back in plenty of time for dinner and feeling elated that we had that time together, silent and distant in words but close and warm in shared experience.

It is a good memory and one I cherish these 46 years later.

Tom

Letters to Mack

About the Author

Tom McCoy is a lifelong fisherman who loves to fly fish for trout but also enjoys all that the saltwater has to offer from his home base on the Long Island Sound to the Florida Keys. He has fished mountain streams north, east, south and west. In this collection he shares these adventures with a lifelong friend named Mack.

"Sometimes you have the good fortune to meet a buddy early on and get to share your life with him" says Tom. "At first it's in school or on the ball field and later through correspondence. Letters at first, then email. This book is a collection of those letters on fishing, hiking and life, featuring trips from Montana to Montauk.

Tom authored his first book *How to Fly Fish for Trout*, when a friend wanted to learn how to fly fish for trout and was overwhelmed by the available instruction manuals. Too much information for a beginner was the problem. The book is written in the familiar style of these stories and truly can get a person started fly fishing for trout (and catching) quicker than most. The Fish Tales chapter has 8 stories to help the new fisherperson digest the lessons.

Letters to Mack, Book One, Correspondence on a fishing Life, a collection of letters on fishing, hiking and life.

Letters to Mack 3: Correspondence from Islamorada to Pulaski includes tarpon and steelhead adventures.

If you enjoyed this book please be so kind as to leave a review on Amazon or Kindle – and tell your friends.

Comments are welcome at
www.tomsfishingstories.com

Books by Tom McCoy:

How to Fly Fish for Trout:
    The First Book to Read

Letters to Mack, Book One:
        Correspondence on a Fishing Life

Letters to Mack 2:
        Correspondence from Montana to Montauk

Letters to Mack 3:
        Correspondence from Islamorada to
        Pulaski

How to Improve Your Fly Fishing & Catching
    30 Fly Fishing Tips & Tactics

All are available on Amazon.com and Kindle.com

More information at www.tomsfishingstories.com

Letters to Mack

http://tomsfishingstories.com

Fishing Journals

Tips & Tactics

Tom's Books & Reviews

The Reading Room

Fish & Friends Gallery

Resources

    Fly Shops

    Lodges

    Guides

    Organizations

Drop me a line

Letters to Mack

TomsFishingStories.com

Letters to Mack

Montana to Montauk

187

Made in the USA
Middletown, DE
06 July 2018